European Immigration and Ethnicity in Latin America

A Bibliography

Oliver Marshall

Institute of Latin American Studies
31 Tavistock Square, London WC1H 9HA

This bibliography was compiled while Oliver Marshall was Research Assistant at the Institute of Latin American Studies.

British Library Cataloguing-in-Publication Data
Marshall, Oliver 1957-
European immigration and ethnicity in Latin America : a bibliography
1. South America. Immigration. History
I. Title
016.980004

ISBN 0-901145-72-6

TABLE OF CONTENTS

European Immigration and Ethnicity in Latin America

Introduction

Over the past two decades a great deal has been published relating to immigrants and their descendants in the United States, Canada, Australia and New Zealand. Promoting officially espoused policies of 'multi-culturalism', Canadian and Australian immigration studies have tended to focus on individual ethnic or national groups, with particular stress laid on patterns of cultural retention or processes of integration. In contrast, Latin America - a region that for much of the period between the mid-nineteenth and mid-twentieth centuries rivalled North America as a destination for European and other immigrants, but where inter-continental immigration is no longer considered a living issue - has not generated the same degree of interest in immigration studies. But where there has been interest, the focus has generally been different. In Latin America immigration has tended to be examined in the context of wider processes of demographic or economic change, while studies relating to individual ethnic groups have to a great extent been the preserve of foreign (mainly European) scholars or local historians. Interests, however, have gradually been converging, influenced in part by the widely held North American ideology of immigrant virtue, by North American patterns of scholarship and by foreign funding. One result has been a steady growth in the body of literature on European immigrant experience in Latin America.

The primary concern when compiling this bibliography has been to list scholarly secondary publications that relate to European immigrants and ethnicity in Latin America since 1800 and that have been published since about 1960 - books, articles in books and journals, working papers and conference proceedings - in all European languages. Latin America here comprises the former Spanish and Portuguese territories in the Americas and also includes Haiti and Belize. With a few exceptions (most notably Mennonites, many of whom arrived in Latin America from Canada, but also Belgians from the Congo, Dutch from Indonesia, French from Algeria and Russians from China whose ethnic identities were more linked to the countries of their ancestors than countries of birth), titles are included only on immigrants arriving directly from Europe itself. Thus, although relating to migration of European *origin*, the now considerable literature on Confederate and other North Americans who settled throughout Latin America, Australians in Paraguay and Afrikaaners in Patagonia (all of European origin), is not listed here unless, as is the case with a few titles, it also has a direct bearing on a particular European immigrant community. Unless they illuminate other aspects of the immigration process or an immigrant community, memoirs and biographies are not listed, nor are publications on European travellers and individual missionaries. However, in trying to include work on as many European immigrant groups in as many Latin American countries of reception as possible, where little or nothing else could be found on a particular group or topic, the general parameters for the consideration of titles have been extended. Even so, with a few exceptions, popular publications (such as travellers' accounts and newspaper and magazine reports) are not included, nor are unpublished works (except North American and British doctoral theses) and primary source material (except guides to sources). Those interested in such publications are advised to consult Juan Bailey and Freya Headlam, *Intercontinental Migration to Latin America: a select bibliography* (London: Institute of Latin American Studies, 1980).

The bibliography's first section lists titles not specific to a particular immigrant group or groups. As almost any discussion dealing with post-independence Argentina and Uruguay, and much of that on other Latin American nations, will have some relevance to the general issue of immigration, it was frequently very difficult to decide what titles to include or exclude. Thus, not infrequently, it was necessary to adopt an almost arbitrary decision on how central the topic of immigration or the focus on Latin America is to the particular publication, in order to determine whether it should be included or not.

Next, the bibliography is divided into sections representing immigrants' national and ethnic backgrounds which, where possible and appropriate, are further divided. Creation of sections and sub-sections was not always easy. Only for 'British and Irish', 'Spanish', and 'Yugoslav' is it possible to create ethnic or national based sub-sections (such as 'English' and 'Welsh', 'Basque' and 'Galician', 'Croat' and 'Slovene'). For other sections, similar sub-sections were not considered appropriate as few of the publications within these main sections were concerned with the immigrants' regional or ethnic origins. As it is, there are numerous titles that fit uneasily in particular sections: for example, convenience, rather than ethnography (or politics), dictate that titles on Corsicans are placed in the 'French' section and that those on Slovaks are placed together with those on Czechs. Publications dealing with several specific groups, where possible, are cross-referenced accordingly.

Sometimes there are overlapping categories, with titles on a particular ethnic group found in more than one section. In such cases, where possible, titles are cross-referenced between sections. Basques are a case in point. For example, in the nineteenth century, Uruguay's considerable 'French' colony largely consisted of Basques. In this case, titles relating to Basques will be found not only in the 'French' section but also in the 'Basque' sub-section of the 'Spanish' section.

The 'German' section also sits extremely awkwardly, a reflection of the fact that to be 'German' is an extremely vague and imprecise concept. German-speakers emigrated to Latin America and elsewhere not only from Germany, but also from Austria, France, Hungary, Poland, Romania, Russia, Switzerland, Yugoslavia and elsewhere across Europe. With Germany as a political entity

iv

only in existence since 1871, German language and culture have traditionally been of much greater importance than country of origin as a basis for ethnic consciousness, despite the paradox that 'Germans' speak what are often mutually incomprehensible dialects. The 'German' section is not divided, being formed mainly of titles on the generic 'German', but also of titles specifically on Volga-Germans, Danube-Suabians, Pommeranians and others. However, titles specifically on Swiss, Austrians and Mennonites form distinct sections (although those nationalities or groups are often referred to in general studies of German immigrants) while, with no ethnographic logic, those on Alsatians are placed in the 'French' section.

Similarly, titles relating to German Jews were not easy to categorise. It was decided to place them in the 'Jewish' list since although they often felt strongly for their German identity, in exile mixing little with other Jews, German Jews were in Latin America because they were Jews and not because they were German. It might have been appropriate to create a German-Jewish sub-section, but it would have stood virtually alone: similar sub-sections would have been difficult for other Jews. Apart from the obvious Sephardi/Ashkenazi division, most studies on Jews in Latin America focus on an amorphous Jewish *community* rather than on *communities*, whether ethnic or class based.

I was not successful in locating titles relating to all European nationalities or ethnic groups, not even all major ones. Some omissions are striking: for example, there are no separate Andorran, Estonian, Romanian or Sammarinese sections even though immigrants from all these countries settled in Latin America. Other sections are disappointingly small, in particular those relating to some of the eastern European nationalities such as Greeks, Latvians, Lithuanians, Russians, Ukrainians and non-Croat Yugoslavs. As far as the eastern nationalities are concerned, there are, of course, many publications on Germans, Jews and Mennonites from the same territories who emigrated to Latin America, but there are still many totally untapped resources for the study of other groups. For example, eastern European immigrants published (and continue to publish) newspapers in many South American countries, while back in Europe periodicals of different kinds were published by national agencies either to promote emigration itself or to maintain contact with overseas populations. Perhaps more surprising is how small the bibliography's 'Portuguese' section is, even allowing for the fact that some significant titles may have been inadvertently omitted. Although well over two million Portuguese (from the mainland, the Azores and Madeira) emigrated to Latin America (mainly to Brazil but also to Argentina, Venezuela and elsewhere) researchers have not afforded them attention in proportion to their numbers. Instead, research relating to Portuguese migration (and Portuguese communities abroad) has concentrated on other areas of the world, most notably on southern Africa, North America and France. Charlotte Erickson applied the term 'the invisible immigrants' to the English and Scots in the United States; the same term would seem appropriate for the Portuguese in Brazil.

Note: Full bibliographical details are given wherever possible. However, for some publications it was not possible to obtain the complete reference (for example, the number of pages or the name of the publisher may be missing). It was decided that these publications should be included despite the missing information.

*   *   *

I would like to express my thanks to all those who have helped in compiling this bibliography. Professor Leslie Bethell, Director of the Institute of Latin American Studies, University of London, offered me the opportunity to compile a bibliography - originally merely a series of references jotted down for my benefit - in a somewhat more systematic way for publication. Alan Biggins, the Institute Librarian was always helpful, especially regarding material related to Argentina, and Valerie Cooper and Pam Decho, Library Assistants, helped track down many obscure references.

Also in London, I would like to thank the staffs of the British Library, the Latvian Library, the Polish Library, the University of London Library and the Wiener Library, and library staff at the Hispanic and Luso-Brazilian Council (Canning House), the Institute of Germanic Studies, the Institute of Historical Research, the London School of Economics and Political Science, the School of Slavonic and East European Studies and University College London. Thanks are due to the staff of New York University's Bobst Library, the New York Public Library, as well as the library staff at the Center for Migration Studies (Staten Island, New York), the Ibero-Amerikanisches Institut (Berlin) and the Institut für Auslandsbeziehungen (Stuttgart), where valuable references were located. I am particularly grateful to the Twenty-Seven Foundation for providing an award enabling me to visit German libraries.

Thanks are owed to the following people who scrutinised preliminary lists for particular nationalities or ethnic groups or who otherwise suggested items for inclusion in the bibliography:

A. Schembri Adami, University of Malta Library, Msida, Malta; Aslaug Agnarsdóttir, University Library, Reykjavik, Iceland; Anne Ainz, National Library of Estonia, Tallinn, Estonia; Onésimo C. Arranz García, Instituto Español de Emigración, Madrid, Spain; Rumen Avramov, Institute of Economics, Bulgarian Academy of Sciences, Sofia, Bulgaria; David Barnwell, Department of Spanish and Portuguese, Columbia University, New York, USA; Alicia Bernasconi, Centro de Estudios Migratorios Latinoamericanos, Buenos Aires, Argentina; Gyula Borbándi, Munich, Germany; Jasna Blažević, Institute for Migration and Nationalities, University of Zagreb, Croatia; Carlos Branco, Secretaria de Estado das Comunidades Portuguesas, Lisbon, Portugal; Gerardo A. Busignani and Luis J.M. Busignani, Asociación de Sanmarineses de la República Argentina, Jujuy, Argentina; Carlos Maria Busignani, Consulado

General de la República de San Marino, Buenos Aires, Argentina; Armelle Chervel, Réseau d'Information sur les Migrations Internationales, Paris, France; Serge Cipko, Department of History, University of Alberta, Edmonton, Canada; Gareth Alban Davies, Aberystwyth, Wales; L.S.E. Dhondt-Willemsen, Emigratiebestuur, 's-Gravenhage, Netherlands; Ivan Dubovický, Department of Ethnography and Folklore, Charles University, Prague, Czechoslavakia; Alfonsas Eidintas, Institute of History, Vilnius, Lithuania; Evelyn Ehrlich, Leo Baeck Institute, New York, USA; Finnbogi Gudmundsson, National Library of Iceland, Reykjavik, Iceland; Liv Heggen, University Library, Oslo, Norway; Robert Owen Jones, Department of Welsh, University College of Swansea, Wales; Martina Kaller, Institute of History, University of Vienna, Austria; Elizabeth Kirwan, National Library of Ireland, Dublin, Ireland; Olavi Koivukangas, Institute of Migration, Turku, Finland; Auvo Kostiainen, Department of History, University of Turku, Finland; Marcin Kula, Warsaw, Poland; Ladislao Kurucz, San Isidro, Argentina; Lúcia Lamounier, Universidade Estadual Paulista, Araraquara, Brazil and Department of Economic and Social History, London School of Economics, England; Birgit Flemming Larsen, Danes Worldwide Archive, Aalborg, Denmark; Joaquim de Costa Leite, Faculdade de Economia, Universidade Nova de Lisboa, Portugal; Colin Lewis, London School of Economics and Institute of Latin American Studies, England; Patrick McKenna, St Patrick's College, Maynooth, Ireland; Luis de Sousa Mello, Arquivo Regional de Madeira, Funchal, Portugal; Gerallt D. Nash, Welsh Folk Museum, Cardiff, Wales; Josef Opatrny, Department of Ethnography and Folklore, Charles University, Prague, Czechoslovakia; Alois Ospelt, Liechtensteinische Landesbibliothek, Vaduz, Liechtenstein; Láslo Ottovay, National Széchényi Library, Budapest, Hungary; Arnd Schneider, Department of Social Anthropology, London School of Economics, England; Jon M. Searle, Garrison Library, Gibraltar; Dorothy Buton Skårdal, Department of American Studies, University of Oslo, Norway; Gunita Štāla, State Library of Latvia, Riga, Latvia; Eddy Stols, Catholic University of Louvain, Belgium; Hans Storhaug, Norwegian Emigration Center, Stavanger, Norway; Emile Thoma, Bibliothèque Nationale de Luxembourg, Luxembourg; Amílcar Tirado, Centro de Estudios Puertorriqueños, Hunter College, The City University of New York, USA; Yngve Turesson, Svenska Emigrantinstitut, Växjö, Sweden; Silvija Vélavičiene, National Library of Lithuania, Vilnius, Lithuania; Timo Virtanen, Institute of Migration, Turku, Finland; Andrej Vovko, Institute for Slovene Emigration Research, Ljubljana, Slovenia; Sara Ward, International Organisation for Migration, Santiago, Chile; Glyn Williams, Department of Sociology and Social Policy, University of Wales, Bangor, Wales; Ulf Zachariasen, The National Library, Tórshavn, Faroe Islands; Art Zailskas, Lithuanian Research and Studies Center, Chicago, USA.

Finally, thanks are owed to Tony Bell and Alison Loader, Institute of Latin American Studies, for their work in preparing the bibliography for publication.

July 1991

PERIODICAL ABBREVIATIONS

AA	American Anthropologist [Washington, DC]
AAAG	Annals of the Association of American Geographers [Washington, DC]
AC	Anales del Caribe [Havana]
ACH	Araucaria de Chile [Madrid]
AE	American Ethnologist [Washington, DC]
AEA	Anuario de Estudios Americanos
AEAT	Anuario de Estudios Atlánticos [Madrid/Las Palmas]
AEH	Anuario de la Escuela de Historia [Rosario]
AFLE	Annali della Fondazione Luigi Einaudi [Turin]
AH	Agricultural History
AHR	American Historical Review [Washington, DC]
AI	Altreitalie [Turin]
AIH	Anales de Investigación Histórica [Río Piedras, PR]
AIP	Anales del Instituto de la Patagonia [Chile]
AJA	American Jewish Archives [Cincinnati]
AJES	American Journal of Economics and Sociology [New York]
AJH	American Jewish History [Waltham, MA]
AJHQ	American Jewish Historical Quarterly [Philadelphia]
AJYB	American Jewish Yearbook [New York and Philadelphia]
AL	América Latina [Moscow]
AM	The Americas [Washington]
AML	América Latina [Rio de Janeiro]
AMP	Anais do Museu Paulista [São Paulo]
AN	Anuario [Rosario]
ANH	Anais de História [São Paulo]
AP	Apuntes [Lima]
AQ	Anthropology Quarterly [Washington, DC]
AR	Arbor: Ciencia, Pensamiento y Cultura [Madrid]
AS	Análise Social [Lisbon]
ASS	American Studies in Scandinavia [Oslo]
AU	An der Ucht [Luxembourg]
AUS	Acta Universitatis Szegediensis (Acta Historica) [Szeged]
AV	Andvari [Reykjavik]
BA	Boletín Americanista [Barcelona]
BABA	Academia: Boletín de la Real Academia de Bellas Artes de San Fernando [Madrid]
BACH	Boletín de la Asociación Cultural Humboldt [Caracas]
BANH/BA	Boletín de la Academia Nacional de la Historia [Buenos Aires]
BANH/Car	Boletín de la Academia Nacional de la Historia [Caracas]
BARSOM	Bulletin de l'Académie Royale des Sciences d'Outre Mer [Brussels]
BBCS	Bulletin of the Board of Celtic Studies [Cardiff]

BCIH	Boletín del Centro de Investigaciones Históricas [Río Piedras, PR]
BELC	Boletín de Estudios Latinoamericanos y del Caribe [Amsterdam]
BEPB	Bulletin d'Etudes Portugaises et Brésiliennes [Paris]
BG	Boletim Geográfico [Rio de Janeiro]
BH	Boletín Histórico [Caracas]
BIEA	Boletín del Instituto de Estudios Asturianos [Oviedo]
BIHAA	Boletín del Instituto de Historia Argentina y Americana [Buenos Aires]
BIHGEP	Boletim do Instituto Histórico, Geográfico e Etnográfico Paranaense [Curitiba]
BIJNPS	Boletim do Instituto Joaquim Nabuco de Pesquisas Sociais [Recife]
BMKS	Bjuletin Mejdunarodno Kulturno Satrudnichestvo [Sofia]
BMRA	Boletín Museo Regional de la Araucaria [Temuco]
BS	Belizean Studies [Belize City]
BZ	Brački zbornik [Split]
CA	Cuadernos Americanos [México, DF]
CAL	Cahiers des Amériques Latines [Paris]
CBP	Comunidade Brasileiro-Polonesa: Anais [Curitiba]
CC	Češi v čizine [Prague]
CG	Cahiers de Géographie [Quebec]
CH	Cuadernos Hispanoamericanos [Madrid]
CHR	Cuadernos de Historia Regional [Buenos Aires]
CINA	Cuadernos del Instituto Nacional de Antropología [Buenos Aires]
CL	Český lid [Prague]
CO	Contenidos [México, DF]
COM	Cahiers d'Outre-Mer [Bordeaux]
CP	Cultura Peruana [Lima]
CR	Caribbean Review [Miami]
CRIAR	Cahiers du CRIAR (Centre de Recherches d'Etudes Ibériques et Ibéro-Américaines) [Rouen]
CT	Commentary [New York]
CS	Caribbean Studies [Río Piedras, PR]
CSO	Cristianismo y Sociedad [México, DF]
CSP	Časopis za suvremenu povijest [Zagreb]
CV	Caravelle: Cahiers du Monde Hispanique et Luso-Brésilien [Toulouse]
CX	Contextos [Montevideo]
DC	Del Caribe [Santiago de Cuba]
DD	Dve domovini (Razprave o izeljenstvu) [Ljubljana]
DE	Demografía y Economía [México, DF]
DEC	Desarrollo Económico [Buenos Aires]
DED	Die evangelische Díaspora
DK	Dubrovnik [Dubrovnik]
DW	Die Warte [Luxembourg]

EC	Echanges [Grenoble]
ECR	Economie Rurale [Paris]
ED/Hav	Economía y Desarrollo [Havana]
EE	Estudos Econômicos [Rio de Janeiro]
EG	Economic Geography [Worcester, MA]
EHR	English Historical Review
EHSEA	Estudios de Historia Social y Económica de América [Madrid]
EI	Economia Internazionale [Genoa]
EIA	Estudos Ibero-Americanos [Porto Alegre]
EK	Ekistiks [Athens]
EL	Estudios Latinoamericanos [Warsaw]
EM	Emigranten [Aalborg]
EML	Estudios Migratorios Latinoamericanos [Buenos Aires]
EP	Estudios Paraguayos [Asunción]
EP	Elders: Periodiek over Emigratie ['s-Gravenhage]
EP	Ethnologia Polona [Warsaw]
EQ	Eugenics Quarterly [Madison, WI]
ERS	Ethnic and Racial Studies [London]
FA	Folklore Americano [México, DF]
FB	De Feelser Babeler [Larochette]
FI	Foro Internacional [México, DF]
FL	Folclore [São Paulo]
FUR	Forum: A Ukrainian Review [Scranton, PA]
GJ	Geographical Journal [London]
GR	Geographical Review [New York]
HA	Historia [Buenos Aires]
HAHR	Hispanic American Historical Review [Durham, NC]
HG	Historic Guelph: Journal of the Guelph Historical Society
HH	Hoy es Historia [Montevideo]
HI	Historia [Santiago]
HM	Historia Mexicana [México, DF]
HO	Hómines [Puerto Rico]
HOLA	Het oude land van Aarschot
HP	Hispania [Baltimore]
HS	Historias [México, DF]
IA	Iberoamérica [Madrid]
IAA	Ibero-Amerikanisches Archiv [Bonn]
IAEA	Inter-American Economic Affairs [Washington, DC]
IAP	Ibero-Americana Pragensia [Prague]
ICM	ICM Latin American Migration Journal [Geneva]
IE	Investigaciones y Ensayos [Buenos Aires]
IER	Irish Ecclesiastical Record [Dublin]
IHR	International History Review [Toronto]
IJPA	International Journal of Psycho-Analysis
ILR	International Labour Review [Geneva]
IMR	International Migration Review [New York]
IM	International Migration [Geneva]

IN	Inmigrantes [Las Breñas]
IP	Istoricheski pregled [Sofia]
IS	The Irish Sword [Dublin]
JBS	Journal of Baltic Studies [Longbeach, CA]
JCG	Journal of Cultural Geography [Bowling Green, OH]
JCH	Journal of Caribbean History [Kingston]
JEH	Journal of Economic History
JEUH	Journal of European History
JGSWGL	Jahrbuch für Geschichte von Staat, Wirtschaft und Gesellschaft Lateinamerikas [Cologne]
JHG	Journal of Historical Geography [London]
JIASWA	Journal of Inter-American Studies and World Affairs [Coral Gables, FL]
JICH	Journal of Imperial and Commonwealth History [London]
JLAS	Journal of Latin American Studies [Cambridge]
JPS	Journal of Peasant Studies [London]
JR	Jewish Review [Buffalo]
JSS	Jewish Social Studies [New York]
JU	Jahrbuch der Ukrainekunde [Munich]
JUS	Journal of Ukrainian Studies [Edmonton]
LAER	NACLA's Latin America and Empire Report [New York]
LAH	Les Amis de l'Histoire [Luxembourg]
LARR	Latin American Research Review
LBR	Luso-Brazilian Review [Madison, WI]
LS	Lateinamerika Studien [Munich]
MA	Mesoamérica [Antigua de Guatemala]
ML	Mennonite Life [Newton, KS]
MQR	Mennonite Quarterly Review [Goshen, IN]
MT	Migracijske teme [Zagreb]
NA	Nova Americana
NCA	The Nineteenth Century and After [London]
NH	Natural History [New York]
NP	Notas de Población [Santiago de Chile]
NS	North-South: Canadian Journal of Latin American Studies
PA	Panorama [La Paz, Baja California Sur]
PAC	Procesos de Articulación Social [Buenos Aires]
PAS	Polish American Studies [Chicago]
PHR	Pacific Historical Review [Los Angeles]
PLG	Profsojuzni letopisi-godshik [Sofia]
PN	Population [Paris]
PP	Past and Present [Oxford]
PPO	Prezeglad Polonijny [Warsaw]
PS	Povijest sporta [Zagreb]
PWA	Polish Western Affairs [Poznań]
QASI	Quadri di Affari Sociali Internazionali [Milan]
QE	Qesher [Tel Aviv]
RA	Revista de Antropologia [São Paulo]
RB	Revista Brasiliense

RBG	Revista Brasileira de Geografia [Rio de Janeiro]
RBH	Revista Brasileira de História [São Paulo]
RBNJM	Revista de la Biblioteca Nacional José Martí [Havana]
RBS	Regio Basiliensis [Basle]
RC	Reconstructionist [Wyncote, PA]
RCA	Revista Colombiana de Antropología [Bogotá]
RCS	Revista de Ciencias Sociales [Río Piedras, PR]
RCH	Revista Chilena de Humanidades [Santiago]
RDS	Revue dejin socialismu [Prague]
REELC	Revista Europea de Estudios Latinoamericanos y del Caribe – European Review of Latin American and Caribbean Studies [Amsterdam]
REMI	Revue Européenne des Migrations Internationales [Poitiers]
RGA	Revista Geográfica Americana [México, DF]
RH	Revista de Historia [Buenos Aires]
RHE	Revista de Historia Económica [Madrid]
RH/SJ	Revista de Historia [San José]
RH/SJu	Revista de Historia [San Juan]
RH/SP	Revista de História [São Paulo]
RHA	Revista de Historia de America [México, DF]
RHAA/Men	Revista de Historia Americana y Argentina [Mendoza]
RHC	Revista de Historia Canaria [Santa Cruz de Tenerife]
RHES	Revista de História Econômica e Social [Lisbon]
RHI	Revue Historique [Paris]
RH/O	Revista de História [Oporto]
RI	Revista de Indias [Madrid]
RIAGP	Revista do Arqueológico e Geográfico de Pernambuco [Recife]
RIB	Revista Interamericana de Bibliografía – Inter-American Review of Bibliography [México, DF]
RICP	Revista del Instituto de Cultura Puertorriqueña [San Juan]
RIEB	Revista do Instituto de Estudos Brasileiros
RIHGB	Revista do Instituto Histórico e Geográfico Brasileiro [Rio de Janeiro]
RIHGSC	Revista do Instituto Histórico e Geográfico de Santa Catarina [Florianópolis]
RIHP	Radovi Instituta za hrvatsku povijest [Zagreb]
RL	Revista Lotería [Panama]
RMP	Revista Museu Paulista [São Paulo]
RPD	Revista Paranaense de Desenvolvimento [Curitiba]
RPS	Revista Paraguaya de Sociología [Asunción]
RSAEF	Revista de la Sociedad Argentina de Estudios Franceses [Buenos Aires]
RSO	Rural Sociology
RV	Revue [Luxembourg]
SA	Sociologia [São Paulo]
SAN	Secolas Annals
SC	Studia Celtica [Cardiff]

SCID	Studies in Comparative International Development [New Brunswick, NJ]
SCR	Studia Croatia [Buenos Aires]
SE	Studi Emigrazione [Rome]
SG	Siglo XIX [Monterrey]
SHG	Studia Historica Gandensia [Ghent]
SJ	Staden-Jahrbuch [São Paulo]
SK	Századok [Budapest]
SM	Siirtolaisuus-Migration [Turku]
SO	Sociológica [Buenos Aires]
SRG	Studi e Ricerche di Geografía
SSR	Sociology and Social Research [Los Angeles]
SSSQ	Southwestern Social Science Quarterly [Austin]
STO	Stimme Österreichs [Vienna]
SZ	Slováci v zahraničí [Bratislava]
TBGAS	Transactions of the Bristol and Gloucestershire Archaeological Society [Bristol]
TC	Trabajos y Comunicaciones [La Plata]
TH	Todo es Historia [Buenos Aires]
TI	Tiszatáj [Szeged]
TL	Theologische Literaturzeitung [East Berlin]
TWBHS	Transactions of the Welsh Baptists Historical Society
U/SF	Universidad [Santa Fe]
UR	Ukrainian Review [London]
VI	Vistazo [Quito]
WHQ	Western Historical Quarterly [Logan, UT]
WHR	Welsh History Review [Cardiff]
WW	Wirtschaftskräfte und Wirtschaftswege [Stuttgart]
YGAS	Yearbook of German-American Studies
YVS	Yad Vashem Studies [Jerusalem]
ZL	Zeitschrift für Lateinamerika [Vienna]
ZR	Zadarska revija [Zadar]

GENERAL STUDIES

Bibliographies

1   BAILEY, Juan and Freya HEADLAM, 1980: *Intercontinental migration to Latin America: a select bibliography.* London: Institute of Latin American Studies, University of London, 65 pp.

2   REY BALMACEDA, Raúl C., 1978: *Comunidades extranjeras en la Argentina: contribución a una bibliografía.* Buenos Aires: Oikos Asociación para la Promoción de los Estudios Territoriales y Ambientales.

General

3   BARNHART, Edward N., 1962: 'Citizenship and political tests in Latin American republics in World War II', *HAHR*, 49/1, pp. 53-79.

4   BERTONI, Lilia Ana and Luis Alberto ROMERO, 1985: 'Aspectos comparativos de la inmigración en el cono sur: la "utopia agraria"', in *La inmigración a América Latina (primeras jornadas internacionales sobre la migración en América).* México, DF: Instituto Panamericano de Geografía e Historia (Serie inmigración, tomo 2), pp. 7-20.

5   BULCOURF, Carlos Gustavo, 1985: 'Noticias desde Europa sobre la inmigración', in *La inmigración a América Latina (primeras jornadas internacionales sobre la migración en América).* México, DF: Instituto Panamericano de Geografía e Historia (Serie inmigración, tomo 2), pp. 33-42.

6   CASES MENDEZ, J.I., 1977: 'Adaptation and integration of highly skilled migrants and their contribution to the economy of developing countries', *IM*, 15/2-3, pp. 191-210.

7   ESTRADA, Baldomero and René SALINAS MEZA, 1987: 'Inmigración europea y movilidad social en los centros urbanos de América Latina (1880-1920)', *EML*, 2/5, pp. 3-27.

8   HASBROUCK, Alfred, 1969: *Foreign legionaires in the liberation of Spanish South America.* New York: Octagon Books [reprint of 1928 edition], 470 pp.

9   HENNESSY, Alistair, 1978: *The frontier in Latin American history.* London: Edward Arnold, 187 pp.

10 HEREDIA, Edmundo A., 1985: 'Notas sobre las migraciones en Hispanoamérica durante las guerras de emancipación', in *La inmigración a América Latina (primeras jornadas internacionales sobre la migración en América).*

México, DF: Instituto Panamericano de Geografía e Historia (Serie inmigración, tomo 2), pp. 97-104.

11   KOEPKE, Wulf, 1983: 'The indios as seen by the European exile writers with an emphasis on exile legend', in Hans-Bernhard Moeller, ed., *Latin America and the literature of exile.* Heidelberg: Carl Winter Universitätsverlag, pp. 151-179.

12   LEWIS, Ward B., 1983: 'Exile drama: the example of Argentina', in Hans-Bernhard Moeller, ed., *Latin America and the literature of exile.* Heidelberg: Carl Winter Universitätsverlag, pp. 233-243.

13   MARSCHALCK, Peter, 1976: 'Social and economic conditions of European emigration to South America in the 19th and 20th centuries', *JGSWGL,* 13, pp. 11-30.

14   MOELLER, Hans-Bernhard, 1983: 'Historical background and patterns of exodus of European exile writers', in Hans-Bernhard Moeller, ed., *Latin America and the literature of exile.* Heidelberg: Carl Winter Universitätsverlag, pp. 49-67.

15   MÖRNER, Magnus, 1985: *Adventurers and proletarians: the story of migrants in Latin America.* Pittsburgh: University of Pittsburgh Press and Paris: UNESCO, 178 pp.

16   RIDINGS, Eugene W., 1985: 'Foreign predominance among overseas traders in nineteenth-century Latin America', *LARR,* 20/2, pp. 3-27.

17   SEGALL, Marcelo, 1983: 'Los europeos en la iniciación del sindicalismo latinoamericano', in *Capitales, empresarios y obreros europeos en América Latina (Actas del 6° Congreso de AHILA, Stockholm, 25-28 de Mayo 1981).* Stockholm: Instituto de Estudios Latinoamericanos (monografías, no. 8, tomo 1), pp. 269-289.

18   SOLBERG, Carl E., 1970: *Immigration and nationalism: Argentina and Chile, 1890-1914.* Austin: University of Texas Press, 233 pp.

19   SZUCHMAN, Mark D., 1983: 'Aliens in Latin America: functions, cycles and reactions', in Hans-Bernhard Moeller, ed., *Latin America and the literature of exile.* Heidelberg: Carl Winter Universitätsverlag, pp. 25-47.

20   THISTLETHWAITE, Frank, 1960: 'Migration from Europe overseas in the nineteenth and twentieth centuries', in *Comité International des Sciences Historiques: XIe Congrès International des Sciences Historiques (Stockholm, 21-27 Août 1960): Rapports V (Histoire Contemporaine).* Gothenburg: Almquist & Wiksell, pp. 32-60.

21   WEIZMANN, H., 1977: 'Rural migration to Latin America: lessons of a recent experience', *IM*, 15/2-3, pp. 243-264.

Argentina

22   ABOU, Sélim, 1981: 'Mythes de l'acculturation aux Etats-Unis et en Argentine', in S. Abou, ed., *L'identité culturelle: relations interethniques et problèmes d'acculturation.* Paris: Editions Anthropos.

23   AUZA, Néstor Tomás, 1990: 'La iglesia argentina y la evangelización de la inmigración', *EML*, no. 14, pp. 105-137.

24   BAILY, Samuel L., 1980: 'Marriage patterns and immigrant assimilation in Buenos Aires, 1882-1923', *HAHR*, 60/1, pp. 32-48.

25   BALCARCE, Mariano, Carlos CALVO and Susana E. SANTOS GÓMEZ, 1985: 'Los representantes argentinos en el extranjero. Su situación en favor de la colonización e inmigración 1855-1885', in *La inmigración a América Latina (primeras jornadas internacionales sobre la migración en América).* México, DF: Instituto Panamericano de Geografía e Historia (Serie inmigración, tomo 2), pp. 135-52.

26   BOLSI, Alfredo S.C., 1980: *Historia del poblamiento en Misiones: inmigración a Oberá entre 1928 y 1975.* Corrientes: Instituto de Investigaciones Geohistóricas (Cuadernos de Geohistoria Regional, no. 1), 48 pp.

27   BONAUDO, Marta, Silvia CROGNOLINO and Elida SONZOGNI, 1988: 'Discusión en torno a la participación política de los colonos santafesinos: Esperanza y San Carlos (1856-1884)', *EML*, no. 9.

28   BORDI DE RAGUCCI, Olga Noemi, 1985: 'La propaganda argentina en Europa como medio de atraer la inmigración 1880-1886', in *La inmigración a América Latina (primeras jornadas internacionales sobre la migración en América).* México, DF: Instituto Panamericano de Geografía e Historia (Serie inmigración, tomo 2), pp. 21-32.

29   BOURDÉ, Guy, 1974: *Urbanisation et immigration en Amérique Latine: Buenos Aires (XIXe et XXe siècles).* Paris: Aubier-Montaigne, 288 pp.

30   CARLINO, Carlos, 1976: *Gauchos y gringos en la tierra ajena.* Buenos Aires: Editorial Plus Ultra, 332 pp.

31   CASTRO, D.S., 1970: *The development of Argentina's immigration policy, 1852-1914.* PhD Thesis, University of California, Los Angeles.

32   CAVIGLIA DE VILLAR, María J., 1984: *Inmigración ultramarina en*

Bahía Blanca. Buenos Aires: Consejo Latinoamericano de Ciencias Sociales, 125 pp.

33   CLEMENTI, Hebe, 1984: *El miedo a la inmigración*. Buenos Aires: Leviatán, 106 pp.

34   CORNBLIT, O., 1967: 'European immigrants in Argentine industry and politics', in C. Véliz, ed., *The politics of conformity in Latin America*. New York: Oxford University Press, pp. 221-48.

35   DELLAROSSA, G., 1978: 'The professional of immigrant descent', *IJPA*, vol. 59, pp. 37-44.

36   DEVOTO, Fernando J., 1989: 'Políticas migratorias argentinas y flujo de población europea (1876-1925)', *EML*, no. 11, pp. 135-158.

37   DÍAZ, Benito, 1975: *Inmigración y agricultura en la época de Rosas*. Buenos Aires: Editorial El Coloquio, 77 pp.

38   DI TELLA, Torcuato S., 1989: 'El impacto inmigratorio sobre el sistema político argentino', *EML*, no. 12, pp. 211-230.

39   DOMINGO, Hugo Luis, 1985: 'El voto político de los extranjeros en la Convención de 1900', in *La inmigración a América Latina (primeras jornadas internacionales sobre la migración en América)*. México, DF: Instituto Panamericano de Geografía e Historia (Serie inmigración, tomo 2), pp. 63-74.

40   DU TOIT, Ben M., 1991: 'Immigration and ethnicity: the case of Argentina', *IM*, 29/1, pp. 77-88.

41   EIDT, Robert C., 1971: *Pioneer settlement in northeast Argentina*. Madison: University of Wisconsin Press, 277 pp.

42   ENSINCK, Oscar Luis, 1979: *Historia de la inmigración y la colonización en la provincia de Santa Fe*. Buenos Aires: Fundación para la Educación, la Ciencia y la Cultura, 359 pp.

43   FISHBURN, Evelyn, 1981: *The portrayal of immigration in nineteenth century fiction (1845-1902)*. Berlin: Colloquium Verlag (Bibliotheca Ibero-Americana), 259 pp.

44   FREUNDLICH DE SEEFELD, R., 1986: 'La integración social de extranjeros en Buenos Aires: según sus pautas matrimoniales. ¿Pluralismo cultural o crisol de razas? (1860-1923)', *EML*, no. 2, pp. 203-231.

45   GALLO, Ezequiel., 1983: *La pampa gringa: la colonización agrícola en*

Santa Fe (1870-1875). Buenos Aires: Sudamericana, 457 pp.

46   GARCÍA, Germán, 1970: *El inmigrante en la novela argentina.* Buenos Aires: Hachette, 108 pp.

47   GERMANI, Gino, 1969: 'Mass immigration and modernization in Argentina', in I.L. Horowitz, J. de Castro and J. Gerassi, eds., *Latin American radicalism.* New York: Random House, pp. 314-55.

48   GODIO, Julio, 1983: 'Migrantes europeos y organización del movimento obrero argentino 1880-1900', in *Capitales, empresarios y obreros europeos en América Latina (Actas del 6° Congreso de AHILA, Stockholm, 25-28 de Mayo 1981).* Stockholm: Instituto de Estudios Latinoamericanos (monografías, no. 8, tomo 1), pp. 314-348.

49   GORI, Gastón, 1964: *Inmigración y colonización en la Argentina.* Buenos Aires: Editorial de la Universidad de Buenos Aires, 103 pp.

50   GONZÁLEZ DE DÍAZ ARAUJO, Graciela, 1985: 'El inmigrante en el teatro argentino (1886-1910)', in *La inmigración a América Latina (primeras jornadas internacionales sobre la migración en América).* México, DF: Instituto Panamericano de Geografía e Historia (Serie inmigración, tomo 2), pp. 85-96.

51   GRINBERG, Leon and Rebecca GRINBERG, 1989: *Psychoanalytic perspectives on migration and exile.* New Haven: Yale University Press, 230 pp.

52   HALPERÍN DONGHI, Tulio, 1976: '¿Para qué la inmigración? Ideología y política inmigratoria y aceleración del proceso modernizador: el caso argentino (1810-1914)', *JGSWL*, vol. 13, pp. 437-489.

53   KORN, Francis, 1965: 'Algunos aspectos de la asimilación de inmigrantes en Buenos Aires, *AML* (April-June), pp. 77-96.

54   KORN, Francis, 1974: *Buenos Aires: los huéspedes del '20.* Buenos Aires: Sudamericana, 215 pp.

55   LATTES, Alfredo E., 1975: 'Migration, population change, and ethnicity in Argentina', in Brian Du Toit and Helen Sofa, eds., *Migration and urbanization: models and adaptation strategies.* The Hague and Paris: Mouton Publishers, pp. 117-142.

56   LATTES, Alfredo E. and Ruth SAUTU, 1978: *Inmigración, cambio demográfico y desarrollo industrial en la Argentina.* Buenos Aires: Centro de Estudios de Población (Cuaderno del CENEP, No. 5), 30 pp.

57   LATTES, Alfredo E., 1990: 'Tratando de asir lo inasible: las dimensiones de la inmigración en la Argentina entre 1945 y el presente', *EML*, no. 15-16, pp. 295-310.

58   LEWIS, Colin, 1987: 'Immigrant entrepreneurs, manufacturing and industrial policy in the Argentine, 1922-1928', *JICH*, 16/1, pp. 77-108.

59   LEWIS, Ward B., 1983: 'Exile drama: the example of Argentina', in Hans-Bernhard Moeller, ed., *Latin America and the literature of exile*. Heidelberg: Carl Winter Universitätsverlag, pp. 233-245.

60   MÍGUEZ, Eduardo J., 1987: 'Política, participación y poder. Los inmigrantes en las tierras nuevas de la Provincia de Buenos Aires en la segunda mitad del siglo XIX', *EML*, nos. 6-7, pp. 337-379.

61   ONEGA, Gladys, 1965: *La inmigración en la literatura argentina, 1880-1910*. Santa Fe: Facultad de Filosofía y Letras, Universidad Nacional del Litoral, 184 pp.

62   OSPITAL, María Silvia, 1985: *Estado e inmigración en la década del 20. La política inmigratoria de los gobiernos radicales*. Buenos Aires: Centro Editor de América Latina (Conflictos y procesos de la historia argentina contemporánea, no. 12), 32 pp.

63   OSPITAL, María Silvia, 1988: 'Fuentes para el estudio de la inmigración en la década 1920 en Argentina', *RIB*, 38/3, pp. 363-382.

64   PANTELIDES, Edith A., 1986: 'Notas respecto a la posible influencia de la inmigración europea sobre la fecundidad de la Argentina', *EML*, no. 3, pp. 351-356.

65   PINTO, Juan, 1964: 'El inmigrante en nuestro teatro', *U/SF*, no. 59. pp. 41-62.

66   PUJOL, Sergio Alejandro, 1984: 'Las revistas culturales de los inmigrantes en Buenos Aires (1914-1930)', *TH*, no. 212, pp. 46-55.

67   RIPA, Julián I., 1987: *Inmigrantes en la Patagonia*. Buenos Aires: Marimar, 164 pp.

68   RODRÍGUEZ, Leopoldo F., 1986: *Inmigración, nacionalismo y fuerzas armadas: antecedentes del golpismo en Argentina, 1870-1930*. México, DF: Editora Internacional, 120 pp.

69   SANTAMARÍA, Daniel, J., 1990: 'Estado, iglesia e inmigración en la Argentina moderna', *EML*, no. 14, pp. 139-181.

70   SENKMAN, Leonardo, 1985: 'Política internacional e inmigración europea en la argentina de postguerra (1945-1948)', *EML*, no. 1, pp. 107-125.

71   SENKMAN, Leonardo, 1988: 'Las relaciones EE.UU.-Argentina y la cuestión de los refugiados de la Post-Guerra: 1945-1948', in *Judaica latinoamericana: estudios histórico-sociales*. Jerusalem: Editorial Universitaria Magnes, Universidad Hebrea, pp. 90-114.

72   SOLBERG, Carl E., 1974: 'Farm workers and the myth of export-led development in Argentina', *AM*, 31/2, pp. 121-138.

73   STAHRINGER DE CARAMUTI, Ofelia I., 1975: *La política migratoria argentina*. Buenos Aires: Ediciones Depalma, 139 pp.

74   SZUCHMAN, Mark D., 1977: 'The limits of the melting pot in urban Argentina: marriage and integration in Córdoba, 1869-1909', *HAHR*, 57/1, pp. 24-50.

75   SZUCHMAN, Mark D., 1986: 'Visions of the melting pot in the American city: European and native expectations in the United States and Argentina in the period of mass immigration', in J.F. Stack, ed., *The primordial challenge: ethnicity in the contemporary world*. New York: Greenwood Press, pp. 43-59.

76   VOGEL, Hans, 1991: 'New citizens for a new nation: naturalization in early independent Argentina', *HAHR*, 71/1, pp. 107-131.

77   WILLIAMS, Glyn, 1978: 'Industrialization and ethnic change in the Lower Chubut Valley, Argentina', *AE*, 5/3, pp. 618-31.

See also: 12; 233; 736

Brazil

78   AZEVEDO, Célia, 1987: *Onda negra, medo branco*. São Paulo: Brasiliense.

79   AZZI, Riolando, 1990: 'O catolicismo de imigração', *EML*, no.14, pp. 5-32.

80   BALHANA, Altiva Pilatti, 1969: 'Política imigratória no Paraná', *RPD*, no. 12, pp. 65-80.

81   BARRETO, F. Menna, 1977: 'Brazil: the integration of highly skilled immigrants and their contribution to social and economic development', *IM*, 15/2-3, pp. 211-219.

82   BEOZZO, José Oscar, 1990: 'As igrejas e a imigração', *EML*, no. 14, pp. 33-79.

83   BONI, Luis A. de, 1980: 'O catolicismo da imigração: do triunfo à crise', in Aldair Marli Lando, ed., *RS*: Imigração e colonização. Porto Alegre: Mercado Aberto, pp. 234-255.

84   BROWNE, George P., 1972: *Government immigration policy in Imperial Brazil, 1822-1870*. PhD Thesis, The Catholic University of America.

85   COSTA, Emilia Viotti da, 1985: *The Brazilian Empire: myths and histories*. Chicago: University of Chicago Press, 287 pp.

86   DEAN, Warren, 1969: *The industrialization of São Paulo, 1880-1945*. Austin: University of Texas Press, 263 pp.

87   DEAN, Warren, 1976: *Rio Claro: a Brazilian plantation system, 1820-1920*. Stanford: Stanford University Press, 234 pp.

88   DELHAES-GUENTHER, Dietrich von, 1987: 'Comportamento procreativo ed emigrazione: la crescita demografica nelle colonie del Brasile meridionale', in Gianfausto Rosoli, ed., *Emigrazioni europee e popolo brasiliano*. Rome: Centro Studi Emigrazione, pp. 168-179.

89   DIEGUES Jr., Manuel, 1964: *Imigração, urbanização e industrialização: estudo sôbre alguns aspectos da contribuição cultural do imigrante no Brasil*. Rio de Janeiro: Centro Brasileiro de Pesquisas Educacionais, 385 pp.

90   FERNANDES, Florestan, 1970: 'Immigration and race relations in São Paulo', in Magnus Mörner, ed., *Race and Class in Latin America*. New York: Columbia University Press, pp. 122-142.

91   FRANCO, Sérgio da Costa, 1959: 'A política de colonização do Rio Grande do Sul', *RB*, no. 25.

92   GRAHAM, Douglas H., 1973: 'Migração estrangeira e a questão da oferta de mão de obra no crescimento econômico brasileiro 1880-1930', *EE*, 3/1, pp. 7-64.

93   GRAHAM, Douglas H. and Thomas W. MERRICK, 1979: *Population and economic development in Brazil, 1800 to the present*. Baltimore and London: The Johns Hopkins University Press, 385 pp.

94   HALL, Michael M., 1969: *The origins of mass immigration in Brazil, 1871-1914*. PhD Thesis, Columbia University.

95   HALL, Michael M., 1974: 'Approaches to immigration history', in Richard Graham and Peter H. Smith, eds., *New approaches to Latin American history*. Austin: University of Texas Press, pp. 175-93.

96   HALL, Michael M., 1975: 'Immigration and the early São Paulo working class', *JGSWGL*, vol. 12, pp. 393-407.

97   HALL, Michael M., 1976: 'Reformadores de classe média no império brasileira: a Sociedade Central de Imigração', *RH/SP*, 53, 105, pp. 147-171.

98   HALL, Michael M. and Verena Martinez STOLKE, 1983: 'The introduction of free labour in São Paulo coffee plantations', *JPS*, 10/2-3, pp. 170-200.

99   HERING, Maria Luiza Renaux, 1987: *Colonização e indústria no Vale do Itajaí: o modelo Catarinense de desenvolvimento*. Blumenau: Editora da FURB, 328 pp.

100   HOLLOWAY, Thomas H., 1978: 'Creating the reserve army? The immigration program of São Paulo 1886-1930', *IMR*, 12/2, pp. 187-209.

101   HOLLOWAY, Thomas H., 1980: *Immigrants on the land: coffee and society in São Paulo, 1886-1934*. Chapel Hill: University of North Carolina Press, 218 pp.

102   HUCK, Hermes Marcelo, 1987: 'A influência do imigrante no processo político brasileiro: o movimento operário-sindical', in Gianfausto Rosoli, ed., *Emigrazioni europee e popolo brasiliano*. Rome: Centro Studi Emigrazione, pp. 136-142.

103   IANNI, Octavio, 1987: *Raças e classes sociais no Brasil*. São Paulo: Editora Brasiliense, 357 pp.

104   KUHN, G., 1975: 'The adaptation and integration of selective immigrants in Brazil. Report on an inquiry', *IM*, 3/4, pp. 208-16.

105   LAMOUNIER, Maria Lúcia, 1988: *Da escravidão ao trabalho livre (a lei de locação de serviços de 1879)*. Campinas: Papirus Editora, 176 pp.

106   LANDO, Aldair Marli, and Eliane C. BARROS, 1980: 'Capitalismo e colonização no Rio Grande do Sul', in Aldair Marli Lando, ed., *RS: Imigração e colonização*. Porto Alegre: Mercado Aberto, pp. 9-46.

107   LAZZARI, Beatriz Maria, 1980: *Imigração e ideologia: reação do parlamento brasileiro à política de colonização e imigração (1850-1875)*. Caxias do Sul: Universidade de Caxias do Sul, 134 pp.

108   LEVINE, Robert M., 1971: 'Some views on race and immigration during

the Old (Brazilian) Republic', *AM*, no. 4, pp. 373-380.

109   MARAM, S.L., 1977: 'The immigrant and the Brazilian labor movement, 1890-1920', in Dauril Alden and Warren Dean, eds., *Essays concerning the socio-economic history of Brazil and Portuguese India*. Gainesville: University Presses of Florida, pp. 178-210.

110   MARAM, Sheldon Leslie, 1979: *Anarquistas, imigrantes e o movimento operário brasileiro*. Rio de Janeiro: Paz e Terra, 180 pp.

111   MARTINS, José de Souza, 1973: *A imigração e a crise do Brasil agrário*. São Paulo: Pioneira, 222 pp.

112   MELO, Evaldo Cabral de, 1984: *O norte agrário e o império 1871-1889*. Rio de Janeiro: Editora Nova Fronteira, 298 pp.

113   MONTEIRO, Norma de Goes, 1973: *Imigração e colonização em Minas, 1889-1930*. Belo Horizonte: Imprensa Oficial, 213 pp.

114   MURILO DE CARVALHO, José, 1981: 'A modernização frustrada: a política de terras no Império', *RBH*, 1/1, pp. 39-57.

115   NEEDELL, Jeffrey D., 1988: *A tropical belle epoque: elite culture and society in turn-of-the-century Rio de Janeiro*. Cambridge: Cambridge University Press, 351 pp.

116   NOGUEIRA, Arlinda Rocha and Lucy Maffei HUTTER, 1975: *A colonização em São Pedro do Rio Grande do Sul durante o Império (1824-1889)*. Porto Alegre: Editora Garatuja, 162 pp.

117   NOGUEIRA, Arlinda Rocha, 1981: 'Como São Paulo hospedava seus imigrantes no início da República', *RIEB*, no. 23, pp. 27-49.

118   PETRONE, Maria Theresa Schorer, 1987: 'Política imigratória e interesses econômicos (1824-1930)', in Gianfausto Rosoli, ed., *Emigrazioni europee e popolo brasiliano*. Rome: Centro Studi Emigrazione, pp. 257-271.

119   PESAVENTO, Sandra Jatahy, 1980: 'O imigrante na política Rio-Grand-ense', in *RS: imigração e colonização*; ed. Aldair Marli Lando. Porto Alegre: Mercado Aberto, pp. 156-194.

120   PIAZZA, Walter F., 1982: *A colonização de Santa Catarina*. Florian-ópolis: Editora Pallotti, 311 pp.

121   SCHRADER, Achim, 1987: 'Minorias étnicas na política educacional do Brasil em torno das escolas de língua estrangeira nos anos 30 e 70', in Gianfausto Rosoli, ed., *Emigrazioni europee e popolo brasiliano*. Rome:

Centro Studi Emigrazione, pp. 323-334.

122   SILVA, José Gentil da, 1983: 'O imigrante como investimento: a propósito do Brasil no princípio do século XIX', in *Capitales, empresarios y obreros europeos en América Latina (Actas del 6° Congreso de AHILA, Stockholm, 25-28 de Mayo 1981)*. Stockholm: Instituto de Estudios Latinoamericanos (monografías, no. 8, tomo 2), pp. 630-656.

123   SKIDMORE, Thomas E., 1974: *Black into white: race and nationality in Brazilian thought*. New York: Oxford University Press, 299 pp.

124   WAIBEL, Leo, 1949: 'Princípios da colonização européia no sul do Brasil', *RBG*, 11/2, pp. 159-217.

125   WAIBEL, Leo, 1950: 'European colonization in southern Brazil', *GR*, vol. 40, pp. 529-547.

126   WEBER, João H., 1980: 'O imigrante na ficção gaúcha', in *RS: imigração e colonização*; ed. Aldair Marli Lando. Porto Alegre: Mercado Aberto, pp. 256-270.

Chile

127   BLANCPAIN, Jean-Pierre, 1981: 'Intelligentsia nationale et immigration européenne au Chili de l'Indépendence à 1914', *JGSWGL*, vol. 18, pp. 249-289.

128   GUTIÉRREZ R., Héctor G., 1979: 'La inmigración española, italiana y portuguesa: Chile 1860-1930', *NP*, 17/48, pp. 61-79.

129   MARTINIC, Mateo, 1975: 'Origen y evolución de la inmigración extranjera en la colonia de Magallanes entre 1870 y 1980', *AIP*, 6/1-2.

130   STABILI, Maria R., 1985: 'Las políticas inmigratorias de los gobiernos chilenos desde la segunda mitad del siglo pasado hasta la década de 1920', *EML*, no. 2, pp. 181-202.

Colombia

131   ARANGO CANO, Jesús, 1951: *Inmigrantes para Colombia*. Bogotá: Librería Voluntad, 126 pp.

Costa Rica

132   HERRERA BALHARRY, Eugenio, 1985: 'Los inmigrantes y el poder en Costa Rica', *RH/SJ*, no. 11, pp. 131-159.

133   MASING, Ulv, 1965: *Foreign agricultural colonies in Costa Rica: an analysis of foreign colonization in a tropical environment.* PhD Thesis, University of Florida.

Cuba

134   CORBITT, D.C. 1942: 'Immigration in Cuba', *HAHR*, vol. 22/2, pp. 240-308.

135   GONZÁLEZ, Dominga, 1988: 'La política inmigratoria en los inicios de la república', *ED/Hav*, Sept./Oct.

136   MOYANO BAZZANI, Eduardo L., 1990: 'Los recursos humanos en la construcción del primer ferrocarril cubano', *AR*, no. 536-537, tomo 136-137, pp. 189-202.

137   VALDÉS BERNAL, Sergio, 1987-88: 'La inmigración en Cuba: estudio lingüístico-histórico', *AC*, pp. 220-239.

Dominican Republic

138   AUGELLI, John P., 1962: 'Agricultural colonization in the Dominican Republic', *EG*, 38, pp. 15-27.

139   GARDINER, C. Harvey, 1979: *La política de inmigración del dictador Trujillo: estudio sobre la creación de una imagen humanitaria.* Santo Domingo: Universidad Nacional Pedro Henríquez Ureña, 237 pp.

140   HOETINK, Harry, 1970: 'The Dominican Republic in the nineteenth century: some notes on stratification, immigration and race', in Magnus Mörner, ed., *Race and class in Latin America.* New York: Columbia University Press, pp. 96-121.

141   WALKER, Malcolm T., 1971: 'Foreign colonists in a Dominican rural community: the costs of economic progress', *CS*, 11/3, pp. 88-98.

Guatemala

142   GRIFFITH, William Joyce, 1965: *Empires in the wilderness: foreign*

colonization and development in Guatemala, 1834-1844. Chapel Hill: University of North Carolina Press, 332 pp.

143   PÉREZ VALENZUELA, Pedro, 1956: *Santo Tomás de Castilla: apuntes para la historia de las colonizaciones en la Costa Atlántica*. Guatemala: Tipografía Nacional, 259 pp.

Haiti

144   PLUMMER, Brenda Gayle, 1984: 'The metropolitan connection: foreign and semiforeign elites in Haiti, 1900-1915', *LARR*, 19/1, pp. 119-142.

Mexico

145   BERNINGER, Dieter George, 1974: *La inmigración en México, 1821-1857*. México, DF: Secretaría de Educación Pública, 198 pp.

146   BERNINGER, Dieter George, 1976: 'Immigration and religious tolerance: a Mexican dilemma, 1821-1860', *AM*, 32/4, pp. 549-565.

147   BRADING, D.A, 1971: *Miners and merchants in Bourbon Mexico, 1763-1810*. Cambridge: Cambridge University Press, 382 pp.

148   CERUTTI, Mario, 1983: 'La formación de capitales preindustriales en Monterrey (1850-1890): Inmigrantes y configuración de una burguesía regional', in *Capitales, empresarios y obreros europeos en América Latina (Actas del 6° Congreso de AHILA, Stockholm, 25-28 de Mayo 1981)*. Stockholm: Instituto de Estudios Latinoamericanos (monografías, no. 8, tomo. 2), pp. 406-435.

149   GONZÁLEZ NAVARRO, Moisés, 1960: *La colonización en México, 1877-1910*. México, DF, 160 pp.

150   HANNA, Alfred and Kathryn HANNA, 1947: 'The immigration movement of the intervention and empire as seen through the Mexican Press', *HAHR*, May, pp. 220-246.

151   SINDICO, Domenico E., 1983: 'Inmigración europea y desarrollo industrial: el caso de Monterrey, México', in *Capitales, empresarios y obreros europeos en América Latina (Actas del 6° Congreso de AHILA, Stockholm, 25-28 de Mayo 1981)*. Stockholm: Instituto de Estudios Latinoamericanos (monografías, no. 8, tomo 2), pp. 436-467.

152   THOMSON, Guy, 1974: 'La colonización en el departamento de Acayucán: 1824-1834', *HM*, 24/2, pp. 253-298.

Paraguay

153   FRETZ, Joseph W., 1962: *Immigrant group settlement in Paraguay: a study in the sociology of colonization*. North Newton, Kansas: Bethel College, 194 pp.

154   HACK, Hendrik, 1958: 'Primavera, a communal settlement of immigrants in Paraguay', *REMP Bulletin* (Royal Tropical Institute, Amsterdam), 13 pp.

155   PIDOUX DE DRACHENBERG, Myra, 1975: 'Inmigración y colonización en el Paraguay, 1870-1970', *RPS*, vol. 12, pp. 65-123.

156   WILLIAMS, John Hoyt, 1977: 'Foreign técnicos and the modernization of Paraguay, 1840-1870', *JIASWA*, 19/2, pp. 233-257.

Peru

157   BONFIGLIO, Giovanni, 1986: 'Introducción al estudio de la inmigración europea en el Perú', *AP*, no. 18, pp. 83-127.

158   DURAND, Francisco, 1988: 'Los primeros industriales y la inmigración extranjera en el Perú', *EML*, no. 9, pp. 198-215.

159   GARCÍA JORDÁN, Pilar, 1989: 'Progreso, inmigración y libertad de cultos en Perú, a mediados del siglo XIX', *CSO*, no. 1.

160   LONGMORE, Thomas Wilson, 1950: *Possibilities of agricultural colonization in Peru with reference to persons of European origin*. PhD Thesis, Michigan State University.

161   RUIZ DE CASTAÑEDA, María Esther, 1990: 'Desarrollo económico y política inmigratoria en el Perú: 1830-1880', *AR*, no. 536-537, tomo 136-137, pp. 143-160.

162   VÁZQUEZ, Mario C., 1970: 'Immigration and mestizaje in nineteenth century Peru', in Magnus Mörner, ed., *Race and class in Latin America*. New York: Columbia University Press, pp. 73-95.

Puerto Rico

163   LUQUE DE SÁNCHEZ, María Dolores, 1988-9: 'Aportaciones y apropiaciones extranjeras: los inmigrantes en la historiografía puertorriqueña', *BCIH*, no. 4, pp. 58-79.

164   SCARANO, Francisco A., 1981: 'Inmigración y estructura de clases: los

hacendados de Ponce, 1815-1845', in Francisco A. Scarano, ed., *Inmigración y clases sociales en el Puerto Rico del siglo XIX*. Río Piedras: Ediciones Huracán.

Uruguay

165   BERETTA CURI, Alcides, 1987: 'El concurso de la inmigración en el desarrollo de una clase empresaria en el Uruguay (1875-1930): los gremios industriales', *EML*, no. 6-7, pp. 181-198.

166   COCCHI, Angel María, Jaime KLACZKO and Juan RIAL ROADE, 1980: 'La urbanización en Uruguay en la época de la inmigración europea', in Frédéric Mauro and Guy Bourdé, eds., *L'industrialisation des pays de la Plata*. Paris: Institut des Hautes Etudes de l'Amérique Latine, pp. 3-32.

167   MORON, I., 1946: *Problemas de la colonización en el Uruguay*. Montevideo: Anales de la Universidad, 249 pp.

168   ODDONE, Juan A., 1966: *La formación del Uruguay moderno: la inmigración y el desarrollo económico-social*. Buenos Aires: Editorial Universitaria de Buenos Aires, 106 pp.

169   ODDONE, Juan A., 1966: *La emigración europea al Río de la Plata; motivaciones y proceso de incorporación*. Montevideo: Editorial de la Banda Oriental, 112 pp.

170   VAINSENCHER, Isaac, 1973: *"No miento ni cedo"*. Montevideo: Editorial ZRIAH, 183 pp.

171   ZUBILLAGA, Carlos, 1989: 'Iglesias e inmigración en el Uruguay moderno', *EML*, no. 11, pp. 179-192.

Venezuela

172   BERGLUND, Susan, 1980: *The "Musiues" in Venezuela: immigration goals and reality, 1936-1961*. PhD Thesis, University of Massachusetts.

173   BERGLUND, Susan, 1982: 'Las bases sociales y económicas de las leyes de inmigración venezolanas, 1831-1935', *BANH/Car*, 65/260, pp. 951-962.

174   BERGLUND, Susan and Humberto HERNÁNDEZ CALIMAN, 1985: *Los de afuera: un estudio analítico del proceso migratorio en Venezuela, 1936-1985*. Caracas: Centro de Estudios de Pastoral y Asistencia Migratoria, 151 pp.

175   KRITZ, Mary M., 1975: 'The impact of international migration on Venezuelan demographic and social structure', *IMR*, vol. 9, winter, pp. 515-543.

176   KRITZ, Mary M., 1985: *20 años de "Musiues". Aspectos históricos, sociológicos y jurídicos de la inmigración europea de Venezuela, 1945-1965.* Caracas: Editorial Sucre, 130 pp.

177   PICOUET, M., A. PELLEGRINO and J. PAPAIL, 1986: 'L'immigration au Vénézuela', *REMI*, 2/2, pp. 25-46.

178   RASMUSSEN, Wayne D., 1947: 'Agricultural colonization and immigration in Venezuela, 1810-1860', *AH*, 21, pp. 155-162.

179   SASSEN-KOOB, Saskia, 1979: 'Economic growth and immigration in Venezuela', *IMR*, 8/3, pp. 455-474.

180   SIEWERS, Enrique, 1939: 'The organisation of immigration and land settlement in Venezuela', *ILR*, 39/6, pp. 764-772, and 40/1, pp. 32-55.

181   TEJERA PARÍS, Enrique, 1987: 'Inmigración: de panacea a dolencia', *BANH/Car*, 70/278, pp. 341-364.

182   TORREALBA, Ricardo [et al], 1983: 'Ciento cincuenta años de políticas inmigratorias en Venezuela', *DE*, no. 3.

183   TROCONIS DE VERACOECHEA, Ermila, 1986: *El proceso de la inmigración en Venezuela.* Caracas: Academia Nacional de la Historia (Colección Fuentes para la Historia Republicana, No. 41), 335 pp.

184   ZAWISZA, Leszek M., 1975: 'Colonización agrícola en Venezuela', *BH*, no. 37, pp. 15-59.

ALBANIAN

Argentina

185 MARQUIEGUI, Dedier Norberto, 1988: 'Aproximación al estudio de la inmigración italo-albanesa', *EML*, no.8, pp. 51-82.

AUSTRIAN

General

186   ASPÖCK, Ruth, 1988: 'Österreichische antifaschistische Gruppen in Lateinamerika', in Friedrich Stadler, ed., *Vertriebene Vernunft II: Emigration und Exil österreichischer Wissenschaft, 1930-1940*. Vienna: Jugend und Volk, pp. 998-1003.

187   GOLDNER, Franz, 1979: 'The Austrian emigration in Latin America', in Franz Goldner, ed., *Austrian emigration, 1938-1945*. New York: F. Ungar Publishing Company, pp. 136-146.

188   ILG, Karl, 1976: 'Die österreichische Emigration nach Südamerika', *ZL*, No. 11, pp. 100-112.

See also: 452

Brazil

189   BENESCH, Leopold, 1947: *Dreizehnlinden. Die Österreichische Siedlung in Brasilien*. Linz: Oberösterreichischer Landesverlag, 120 pp.

190   FERSMANN, Andreas P., 1988: 'Exilland Brasilien. Aperçu zur literarischen Emigration', in Friedrich Stadler, ed., *Vertriebene Vernunft II: Emigration und Exil österreichischer Wissenschaft, 1930-1940*. Vienna: Jugend und Volk, pp. 1012-1016.

191   HINNER, Rudolf Robert, 1966: 'Die österreichische Siedlung Dreizehnlinden in Santa Catarina', *SJ*, vol. 14, pp. 121-126.

192   ILG, Karl, 1982: *Heimat Südamerika. Brasilien und Peru*. Innsbruck and Vienna: Tyrolia-Verlag, 287 pp.

Chile

193   KINZEL KAHLER, Enrique, 1975: *100 Años Nueva Braunau. Historia y progreso*. Santiago, 58 pp.

194   WINKELBAUER, Waltraud, 1988: *Die österreichisch-chilenischen Beziehungen vom Vormärz bis zum Ende der Habsburgermonarchie*. Cologne and Vienna: Böhlau Verlag, 256 pp.

Mexico

195 KOYBER, Christian, 1988: 'Einige Anmerkungen zum Exil österreichischer Intellektueller in Mexiko 1938 bis 1945', in Friedrich Stadler, ed.,
*Vertriebene Vernunft II: Emigration und Exil österreichischer Wissenschaft,
1930-1940.* Vienna: Jugend und Volk, pp. 1004-1011.

See also: 1012

Peru

196 SCHMID-TANNWALD, Karl, 1957: *Pozuzo. Vergessen im Urwald.*
Brauschweig: Westermann, 262 pp.

197 VANCSA, O., 1964: 'Pozuzo, wahrscheinlich die älteste österreichische
Kolonie'. *STO*, No. 13.

See also: 192; 605; 609; 610

BELGIAN

General

198   EVERAERT, John, 1976: 'El movimento emigratorio desde Amberes a América Latina durante el siglo XIX (1830-1914). Una estadística provisoria', *JGSWGL*, vol. 13, pp. 331-360.

199   EVERAERT, John, 1977: 'De Belgische emigratie naar Latijns-Amerika tijdens de XIXde eeuw (1830-1914). Socio-demografische analyse van een voorlopige statistiek', *SHG*, No. 200 pp. 83-116.

200   EVERAERT, John, 1979: 'Emigración desde Amberes a América Latina. Fuentes y estado de investigación', in *La emigración europea a la América Latina: fuentes y estado de investigación (informes presentados a la IV Reunión de Historiadores Latinoamericanistas Europeos)*. Berlin: Colloquium Verlag (Bibliotheca Ibero-Americana), pp. 165-179.

201   STENGERS, Jean, 1978: *Emigration et immigration en Belgique au XIXe et au XXe siècles*. Bruxelles: Académie Royale des Sciences d'Outre-Mer, 107 pp.

202   STOLS, Eddy, 1976: 'Penetração econômica, assistência técnica e "brain drain": aspectos da emigração Belga para a América Latina por volta de 1900', *JGSWGL*, vol. 13, pp. 361-385.

203   STOLS, Eddy, 1979: 'L'expansion belge en Amérique Latine vers 1900', *BARSOM*, pp. 100-135.

204   STOLS, Eddy, 1983: 'Capitais, empresários e operários belgas nos processos de industrialização da América Latina', in *Capitales, empresarios y obreros europeos en América Latina (Actas del 6º Congreso de AHILA, Stockholm, 25-28 de Mayo 1981)*, Stockholm: Instituto de Estudios Latinoamericanos (monografías, no. 8, vol. 1), pp. 13-30.

205   STOLS, Eddy, 1985: 'Emigratie en immigratie in historisch perspectief', in Albert Martens and Frank, eds., *Moulaert Binnenlandse minderheden in Vlaanderen-België*. Antwerp and Amsterdam: De Nederlandsche Boekhandel, pp. 123-144.

Argentina

206   CAMERLINCKX, 1973: 'Vlaamse Families in Argentina tussen 1880 en

1910', *HOLA*, vol. 8, pp. 145-160.

207 DI FILIPPO, Josefina, 1982: 'Inmigración belga calificada en el siglo XIX', *SO*, no. 9, pp. 115-125.

208 STOLS, Eddy, 1978: 'Colonisation et intérêts belges en Argentine (1830-1914)', *WW*, 4, pp. 287-312.

See also: 209

Brazil

209 EVERAERT, John, 1980: 'La imagen de América Latina en Bélgica durante el siglo XIX (1835-1890). Idealización y demistificación del Brasil y de la Argentina', *EL*, no. 6, pt. 1, pp. 89-104.

210 FICKER, C., 1972: *Charles van Lede e a colonização belga em Santa Catarina. Subsídios para a história de colonização de ilhota, no rio Italaíaçu, pela "Compagnie belge-brésilienne de colonisation"*. Blumenau, 38 pp.

211 MELLO, José Antonio Gonsalves de, 1959: 'Trabalhadores belgas em Pernambuco (1859-1863)', *BIJNPS*, no. 8, pp. 13-37.

212 STOLS, Eddy, 1987: 'Les Belges au Mato Grosso et Amazonie ou la récidive de l'aventure congolaise, 1895-1914', in M. Dumoulin and E. Stols, eds., *La Belgique et l'étranger aux XIXème et XXème siècles*. Brussels and Louvain la Neuve: Recueil de Travaux d'Histoire et de Philologie (6e série, Fascicule 33), pp. 77-112.

Guatemala

213 EVERAERT, John, 1983: 'Colonisation "agricole" et sous-développement en Amérique Centrale. L'expérience belge de Santo-Tomás de Guatemala (1842-1856)', in *Atti della X settimana di studio di prato* (Firenze), pp. 661-685.

214 FABRI, Joseph, 1955: *Les belges au Guatémala, (1840-1845)*. Brussels: Académie Royale des Sciences Coloniales, 266 pp.

215 LEYSBETH, Nicolas, 1938: *Historique de la colonisation belge à Santo-Tomás, Guatemala*. Brussels: Nouvelle Société d'Éditions, 359 pp.

See also: 142; 143

BRITISH and IRISH

General

216   BLAKEMORE, Harold, 1979: 'La emigración británica a América Latina en los siglos XIX y XX', in *La emigración europea a la América Latina: fuentes y estado de investigación (informes presentados a la IV Reunión de Historiadores Latinoamericanistas Europeos)*. Berlin: Colloquium Verlag (Bibliotheca Ibero-Americana), pp. 137-151.

217   GREENHILL, Robert, 1977: 'Merchants and the Latin American trades: an introduction', in D.C.M. Platt, ed., *Business imperialism, 1840-1930: an inquiry based on British experience in Latin America*. Oxford: Oxford University Press, pp. 159-197.

218   PLATT, D.C.M., 1964: 'British agricultural colonization in Latin America: Part 1', *IAEA*, 18/3, pp. 3-38.

219   PLATT, D.C.M., 1965: 'British agricultural colonization in Latin America: Part 2', *IAEA*, 19/1, pp. 23-42.

220   PLATT, D.C.M., 1973: 'The British in South America: an archive report', in Peter Walne, ed., *A guide to manuscripts for the history of Latin America and the Caribbean in the British Isles*. Oxford: Oxford University Press, pp. 495-513.

221   STANG, Gudmund, 1983: 'Aspectos de la política de personal de las empresas británicas en América Latina 1880-1930', in *Capitales, empresarios y obreros europeos en América Latina (Actas del 6° Congreso de AHILA, Stockholm, 25-28 de Mayo 1981)*, Stockholm: Instituto de Estudios Latinamericanos (monografías, no. 8, vol. 2), pp. 501-550.

Argentina

222   BAILEY, John P., 1976: *The British in Argentina*. PhD Thesis, University of Surrey.

223   BAILEY, John P., 1978: *Immigration and ethnic relations: the British in Argentina*. Bundoora: La Trobe University (La Trobe Sociology Papers, no. 44), 29 pp.

224   BAILEY, John P., 1979: 'Inmigración y relaciones étnicas: los ingleses en la Argentina', *DEC*, 18/72, pp. 539-558.

225   FOULKES, Haroldo, 1983: *Los Kelpers en las Malvinas y en la Patagonia*. Buenos Aires: Ediciones Corregidor, 139 pp.

226   GRAHAM-YOOLL, Andrew, 1981: *The forgotten colony: a history of the English speaking communities in Argentina*. London: Hutchinson, 318 pp.

227   HENNESSY, Alistair, 1991: 'Argentinians, Anglos and others', in Alistair Hennessy and John King, eds., *The land that England lost: essays on the British Argentine connection*. London: Lester Crook Academic, pp. 1-46.

228   JAKUBS, Deborah D., 1986: *A community of interests: social history of the British in Buenos Aires, 1860-1914*. PhD Thesis, Stanford University.

229   JAKUBS, Deborah D., 1987: 'Straddling the fence no more: the Falkland/Malvinas War and its impact on the Anglo-Argentine Identity', in *Seminar on the Acquisition of Latin American Library Materials (SALALM). Papers of the thirty-first annual meeting*. Madison: University of Wisconsin, pp. 100-106.

230   JONES, Wilbur Devereaux, 1960: 'The Argentine British colony in the times of Rosas', *HAHR*, 40/1, pp. 90-97.

231   MARSHALL, Oliver, 1991: 'Peasants or planters? British pioneers on Argentina's tropical frontier', in Alistair Hennessy and John King, eds., *The land that England lost: essays on the British Argentine connection*. London: Lester Crook Academic, pp. 141-156.

232   MÍGUEZ, Eduardo José, 1984: 'Inversiones familiares británicas en tierras argentinas (1850-1914)', *RI*, 41/165-166, pp. 637-674.

233   MÍGUEZ, Eduardo José, 1985: *Las tierras de los ingleses en la Argentina, 1870-1914*. Buenos Aires: Editorial de Belgrano, Buenos Aires, 348 pp.

234   MONACCI, Gustavo A., 1979: *La colectividad británica en Bahía Blanca*. Bahía Blanca: Universidad Nacional del Sur, 152 pp.

235   REBER, Vera Blinn, 1979: *British mercantile houses in Buenos Aires, 1810-1880*. Cambridge, Mass.: Harvard University Press, 206 pp.

Brazil

236   EAKIN, Marshall C., 1989: *British enterprise in Brazil. The St. John d'el Rey Mining Company and the Morro Velho gold mine, 1830-1960*. Durham and London: Duke University Press, 334 pp.

237   FREYRE, Gilberto, 1942: *Inglêses*. Rio de Janeiro: José Olympio, 175 pp.

238   FREYRE, Gilberto, 1948: *Inglêses no Brasil: aspectos da influência britânica sobre a vida, a paisagem e a cultura do Brasil.* Rio de Janeiro: José Olympio, 394 pp.

239   GRAHAM, Richard, 1968: *Britain and the onset of modernization in Brazil (1850-1914).* Cambridge: Cambridge University Press, 384 pp.

240   RIOPARDENSE DE MACEDO, F., 1975: *Inglêses no Rio Grande do Sul.* Pôrto Alegre, 116 pp.

241   WATTS, Alfredo J., 1944: 'A colônia inglêsa em Pernambuco', *RIAGP*, vol. 39.

Chile

242   CAVIERES P., Eduardo: *Chilean trade and British traders, 1820-79.* PhD Thesis, Essex University.

243   FERNÁNDEZ, Manuel A., 1978: *The development of the Chilean economy and its British connections, 1895-1914.* PhD Thesis, University of Glasgow.

244   FERNÁNDEZ, Manuel A., 1983: 'Merchants and bankers: British direct and portfolio investment in Chile during the nineteenth century', *IAA*, vol. 9, pp. 349-379.

245   KINSBRUNER, Jay, 1970: 'The political influence of British merchants resident in Chile during the O'Higgins administration, 1817-1823', *AM*, 27/1, pp. 26-39.

246   MAYO, John, 1987: *British merchants and Chilean development, 1851-1886.* Boulder and London: Westview Press, 272 pp.

247   MAYO, John, 1987: 'The British community in Chile before the nitrate age', *HI*, no. 22, pp. 135-150.

248   MONTEON, Michael, 1975: 'The British in the Atacama Desert: the cultural bases of economic imperialism', *JEH*, 35/1, pp. 117-133.

249   ZIMMERMAN, Daniel W., 1977: *British influence in the modernization of Chile, 1860-1914.* PhD Thesis, University of New Mexico.

Costa Rica

250   MURCHIE, Anita Gregorio, 1980: *Imported spices: a study of Anglo-*

American settlers in Costa Rica, 1821-1900. San José: Ministerio de Cultura, 344 pp.

Guatemala

See: 142; 143

Mexico

251   TENENBAUM, Barbara, 1979: 'Merchants, money, and mischief: the British in Mexico, 1821-1862', *AM*, 35/3, pp. 317-339.

Paraguay

252   PLÁ, Josefina, 1970: 'Los británicos en el Paraguay I', *RHA*, pp. 340-371.

253   PLÁ, Josefina, 1971: 'Los británicos en el Paraguay II', *RHA*, pp. 21-60.

254   PLÁ, Josefina, 1976: *The British in Paraguay, 1850-1870.* Richmond (Surrey): Richmond Publishing Company, 277 pp.

See also: 154; 156

Peru

255   HARRIMAN, Brenda, 1984: *The British in Peru.* Lima, 124 pp.

256   MILLER, Rory, 1979: *British business in Peru, 1883-1930.* PhD Thesis, Cambridge University.

Uruguay

257   HIRST, Lloyd, 1975: *Britons at Maldonado.* Montevideo: Ediciones Géminis, 149 pp.

Cornish

Mexico

258   HERRERA CANALES, Inés, Cuauhtémoc VELASCO ÁVILA, and Eduardo FLORES CLAIR, 1983: 'Los aliados del capital. Trabajadores

ingleses en Real de Monte y Pachuca en el siglo XIX', *HS*, no. 3, pp. 69-76.

259   HERRERA CANALES, Inés, Cuauhtémoc VELASCO ÁVILA, and Eduardo FLORES CLAIR, 1981: *Etnia y clase: los trabajadores ingleses de la Compañía Real de Monte, 1824-1906*. México, DF: Departamento de Investigaciones Históricas, INAH (Cuadernos de Trabajo, no. 38), 76 pp.

English

Brazil

260   HORN, Pamela L.R., 1970: 'Gloucestershire and the Brazilian emigration movement: 1872-73', *TBGAS*, vol. 89, pp. 167-174.

Paraguay

261   HERKEN-KRAUER, Juan Carlos, 1981: 'La inmigración en el Paraguay de posguerra: el caso de los "Lincolnshire Farmers" (1870-1873)', *RPS*, 18/52, pp. 33-107.

262   WARREN, Harris Gaylord, 1965: 'The "Lincolnshire Farmers" in Paraguay: an abortive emigration scheme of 1872-1873', *AM*, pp. 243-62.

Venezuela

263   HANNA, Alfred Jackson and Kathryn Abby HANNA, 1960: *Confederate exiles in Venezuela*. Tuscaloosa, Alabama: Confederate Publishing Company (Confederate Centennial Studies, No. 15), 149 pp.

Irish

General

264   IRELAND, J. de Courcy, 1952-3: 'Irish soldiers and seamen in Latin America', *IS*, 1/4, pp. 296-302.

Argentina

265   COGHLAN, Eduardo, 1970: *Los irlandeses. Apuntes para la historia y la genealogía de las familias irlandesas establecidas en la República Argentina en el siglo XIX*. Buenos Aires: The Southern Cross, 31 pp.

266   COGHLAN, Eduardo, 1982: *El aporte de los irlandeses a la formación de la nación argentina*. Buenos Aires: Librería Alberto Casares, 670 pp.

267   COGHLAN, Eduardo, 1987: *Los irlandeses en la Argentina: su actuación y descendencia*. Buenos Aires: Librería Alberto Casares, 964 pp.

268   KEOGH, K., 1991: 'Argentina and the Falklands/Malvinas: the Irish connection', in Alistair Hennessy and John King, eds., *The land that England lost: essays on the British Argentine connection*. London: Lester Crook Academic, pp. 123-140.

269   KOROL, Juan Carlos and Hilda SÁBATO, 1981: *Cómo fue la inmigración irlandesa en Argentina*. Buenos Aires: Editorial Plus Ultra, 214 pp.

270   MURRAY, Thomas, 1919: *The story of the Irish in Argentina*. New York: P.J. Kennedy & Sons, 512 pp.

271   SÁBATO, Hilda, 1991: *Agrarian capitalism and the world market: Buenos Aires in the pastoral age, 1840-1890*. Albuquerque: University of Mexico Press, 320 pp.

272   USSHER, James M., 1948: 'Irish immigrants in Argentina', *IER*, 5th ser., vol. 70, pp. 385-392.

273   USSHER, James [Santiago], 1951: *Father Fahy. A biography of Anthony Dominic Fahy, O.P. Irish missionary in Argentina (1805-1871)*. Buenos Aires, 213 pp.

274   USSHER, James [Santiago], 1952: *Padre Fahy. Biografía de Antonio Domingo Fahy, O.P. Misionero irlandés en la Argentina (1805-1871)*. Buenos Aires, 219 pp.

275   USSHER, James [Santiago], 1954: *Los capellanes irlandeses en la colectividad hiberno-argentina durante el siglo XIX*. Buenos Aires, 239 pp.

276   USSHER, James [Santiago], 1955: *Las Hermanas de la Misericordia (Irlandesas): apuntes históricos sobre sus cien años en la Argentina*. Buenos Aires, 146 pp.

Brazil

277   ALLENDORFER, Frederic von, 1957: 'An Irish regiment in Brazil, 1826-28', *IS*, 3/10, pp. 28-31.

278   IRELAND, J. de Courcy, 1958: 'Note on an Irish regiment in Brazil', *IS*, 3/12, pp. 205-6.

279   LAUTH, Aloisius Carlos, 1987: *A Colônia Príncipe Dom Pedro: um caso de política imigratória no Brasil Império*. Brusque: Museu Arquidiocesano Dom Joaquim, 110 pp.

Mexico

280   MILLER, Robert Ryal, 1989: *Shamrock and sword: the Saint Patrick's Battalion in the U.S.-Mexican War*. Norman and London: University of Oklahoma Press, 232 pp.

Scottish

General

281   FERNÁNDEZ, Manuel A., 1985: 'The Scots in Latin America: a survey', in R.A. Cage, ed. *The Scots abroad: labour, capital, enterprise, 1750-1914*. London: Croom Helm, pp. 220-250.

Argentina

282   GRIERSON, Cecilia, 1925: *Colonia de Monte Grande, Provincia de Buenos Aires. Primera y única colonia formada por escoceses en la Argentina*. Buenos Aires, 68 pp.

283   MAINWARING, Michael J., 1983: *From the Falklands to Patagonia: the story of a pioneer family*. London: Allison & Busby, 288 pp.

Venezuela

284   RHEINHEIMER, Hans P., 1988: *Topo: the story of a Scottish colony near Caracas 1825-1827*. Edinburgh: Scottish Academic Press, 167 pp.

285   VAUGHAN, Edgar, 1979: 'The Guayrians at Guelph in Upper Canada. Scottish settlers for Canada from Venezuela. A bureaucratic problem in 1827', *HG*, vol. 18, 112 pp.

Welsh

Bibliography

286   WILLIAMS, Glyn, 1979: *The Welsh in Patagonia: a critical bibliographic*

review. Cardiff: University of Wales Press, 174 pp.

Argentina

287   ARCE, José, 1965: *Roca y los galeses del Chubut.* Buenos Aires: Museo Roca, 26 pp.

288   BAUR, John E., 1954: 'The Welsh in Patagonia: an example of nationalistic migration', *HAHR*, vol. 34, pp. 468-492.

289   BOWEN, E.G., 1966: 'The Welsh Colony in Patagonia 1865-1895. A study in historical geography', *GJ*, 132/1, pp. 16-31.

290   DAVIES, Gareth Alban, 1976: *Tan Tro Nesaf: Darlum o Wladfa Gymreig Patagonia.* Llandysul: Gwasg Gomer, 156 pp.

291   GEORGE, W.R.P., 1972: *Gyfaill Hoff.* Llandysul: Gwasg Gomer, 241 pp.

292   GREEN, Fred, 1984: *Pethau Patagonia.* Pen-y-groes: Cyhoeddiadau Mei, 124 pp.

293   JONES, Mathew Henry and Alberto ABDALA, 1965: *Centenario de la colonización galesa del Chubut, 1865-1965. Capillas del Valle.* Trelew.

294   JONES, Robert Owen, 1973-74: 'Amrywiadau Geirfaol yng Nghymraeg y Wladfa', *SC*, vols. 8-9, pp. 287-98.

295   JONES, Robert Owen, 1975: 'Crefydd a'r Bedyddwyr yn y Wladfa', *TWBHS*, pp. 5-16.

296   JONES, Robert Owen, 1976-8: 'Cydberthynas Amrywiadau Iaith a Nodweddion Cymdeithasol yn y Gaiman, Chubut', *BBCS*, 27/1, pp. 51-64.

297   JONES, Robert Owen, 1979: *Tyred Drosodd – Safiad y Wladfa.* [Caernarfon]: Gwynedd County Library Publication, 38 pp.

298   JONES, Robert Owen, 1984: 'Change and variation in the Welsh of Gaimán, Chubut', in M.J. Ball and G.G. Jones, eds., *Welsh phonology, selected readings.* Cardiff: University of Wales Press, pp. 237-261.

299   JONES, Robert Owen, 1983-84: 'Amrywiaeth tafodieithol a phatrwm newid ieithyddol yng Nghymraeg y Wladfa', *SC*, vols. 18-19, pp. 253-267.

300   JONES, Robert Owen, 1983: *Astudiaeth o Gydberthynas Nodweddion Cymdeithasol ag Amrywiadau'r Gymraeg yn y Gaiman, Dyffryn y Camwy.* PhD Thesis, University College of Swansea.

301   JONES, Robert Owen, 1986: 'Language variation and social stratification in the Welsh community of Gaimán', in G.W. MacLennan, ed., *Proceedings of the first North American Congress of Celtic Studies* (University of Ottawa, 26-30 March 1986), pp. 481-98.

302   JONES, Robert Owen, 1987: *Yr Efengyl yn y Wladfa*. Bridgend: Llyfrgell Efengylaidd Cymru, 56 pp.

303   JONES, Robert Owen, 1987: 'Diffusion of linguistic change', in N. Boretzky, W. Enninger, T. Stolz, eds., *Beitrage zum 3 Essener Kolloquium über Sprachwandel und seine bestimmenden Factoren.* pp. 163-184.

304   JONES, Robert Owen, 1988: 'Language variation and social stratification: linguistic change in progress', in M.J. Ball, ed., *The use of Welsh: a contribution to sociolinguistics.* Cleveden and Philadelphia: Multilingual Matters, pp. 284-306.

305   JONES, Robert Owen, 1989: 'From Patagonia to Saskatchewan. An attempt to secure a separate Welsh linguistic and cultural identity', in C. Byrne, ed., *Proceedings of the second North American Congress of Celtic Studies* (Halifax, 16-19 August 1989).

306   JONES, Valmai, 1985: *Atgofion am y Wladfa*. Llandysul: Gwasg Gomer, 130 pp.

307   MARTÍNEZ RUIZ, Bernabé, 1977: *La colonización galesa en el valle del Chubut.* Buenos Aires: Editorial Galerna, 151 pp.

308   OWEN, Geraint Dyfnallt, 1977: *Crisis in Chubut: a chapter in the history of the Welsh colony in Patagonia.* Swansea: Christopher Davies, 161 pp.

309   POLLOCK, Norman, 1980: 'The English in Natal and the Welsh in Patagonia', in A. Lemon and N. Pollock, eds., *Studies in overseas settlement and population.* London and New York: Longman, pp. 207-224.

310   POWELL, R.D., 1979: *Politics of agricultural settlement: the case of the Welsh in Chubut.* PhD Thesis, McGill University, Montreal.

311   THOMAS, Lewis H., 1973: 'Welsh settlement in Saskatchewan, 1902-1914', *WHQ*, 4/4, pp. 435-449.

312   WILLIAMS, Glyn, 1968: 'Incidence and nature of acculturation within the Welsh colony of Chubut: a historical perspective', in *Papers of the Kroeber Anthropological Society*, no. 39, pp. 72-87.

313   WILLIAMS, Glyn, 1969: 'Welsh contributions to the exploration of Patagonia', *GR*, 135/2, pp. 213-27.

314   WILLIAMS, Glyn, 1975: *The desert and the dream: a study of Welsh colonization in Chubut, 1865-1915*. Cardiff: University of Wales Press, 230 pp.

315   WILLIAMS, Glyn, 1976: 'La emigración galesa a la Patagonia, 1865-1915', *JGSWGL*, vol. 13, pp. 239-292.

316   WILLIAMS, Glyn, 1976: 'The structure and process of Welsh emigration to Patagonia', *WHR*, 8/1, pp. 42-74.

317   WILLIAMS, Glyn, 1978: 'Industrialization and ethnic change in the Lower Chubut Valley, Argentina', *AE*, 5/3, pp. 618-631.

318   WILLIAMS, Glyn, 1978: 'Cwm Hyfryd: a Welsh settlement in the Patagonian Andes', *WHR*, 9/1, pp. 57-83.

319   WILLIAMS, Glyn, 1979: 'Welsh settlers and Native Americans in Patagonia', *JLAS*, 2/1, pp. 41-66.

320   WILLIAMS, Glyn, 1980: 'La imagen sobre América Latina en Gales durante los siglos XIX y XX', *EL*, no. 6, pp. 363-383.

321   WILLIAMS, Glyn, 1991: 'Neither British nor Argentinian: the Welsh in Patagonia', in Alistair Hennessy and John King, eds., *The land that England lost: essays on the British Argentine connection*. London: Lester Crook Academic, pp. 109-122.

322   WILLIAMS, Glyn, 1991: *The Welsh in Patagonia: the state and the ethnic community*. Cardiff: University of Wales Press, 280 pp.

323   WILLIAMS, R. Bryn, 1962: *Y Wladfa*. Cardiff: University of Wales Press, 334 pp.

324   WILLIAMS, R. Bryn, 1980: *Atgofion o Batagonia*. Llandysul: Gwasg Gomer, 138 pp.

325   WILLIAMS, R. Bryn, 1965: *Gwladfa Patagonia. The Welsh in Patagonia*. Cardiff: University of Wales Press, 77 pp.

See also: 40; 77

Brazil

See: 320

BULGARIAN

General

326 ALEKSANDROVA, Maria, 1979: 'Kulturni proiavi na bulgari v Latinska Amerika predi 9.09.1944', *BMKS*, II seriia, no. 2.

327 ALEKSANDROVA, Maria, 1984: 'Revoliutsionnata deinost na bulgarskite emigranti v Latinska Amerika i borbite na latinoamerikanskiia proletariat, otrazeni v bulgarskiia rabotnicheski pechat (1891-1944)', *PLG*, no. 13.

328 GONEVSKI, Khristo, 1980: *Daleche ot roden krai (Spomeni ot Arzhntina).* Sofia: Partizdat.

329 PETROV, Dimitur, and NIKOLOV, Tsvetan, 1988: *Bulgari v Iuzhna Amerika.* Sofia: Partizdat, 184 pp.

Argentina

330 AVRAMOV, Rumen, 1986: 'Bulgarskata emigratsiia v Arzhentina 1900-1940', *IP*, no. 6.

331 AVRAMOV, Rumen, 1990: 'La emigración búlgara en Argentina (1900-1940)', *EL*, no. 13, pp. 225-256.

332 ALEKSANDROVA, Maria, 1987: 'Bulgaro-arzhentinski vruzki (1906-- 1949)', *IP*, no. 3, pp. 35-47.

333 GEORGIEV, Nikolai, 1965: *Bulgari v Iuzhna Amerika.* Sofia: Otechestven Front.

334 MICHOFF, Jorge, 1975: 'De los Balcanes al Chaco', *IN*, no. 2, pp. 40-44.

335 MICHOFF, Jorge, 1979: 'Aporte de la colectividad búlgara al acervo cultural argentino y chaqueño', *IN*, no. 6.

See: 328

Paraguay

See: 1437

CZECH AND SLOVAK

General

336 BAĎUROVÁ, Anežka, 1983: 'Comienzos de la historia de las revistas compatriotas checoslovacas en América Latina, 1902-1923', *IAP*, yr. 17, pp. 279-289.

337 KAŠPAR, Oldřich., 1986: 'Přírodovědec Tadeáš Haenke a počátky českého vystěhovalectví do Latinské Ameriky', *CC*, no. 1, pp. 165-178.

338 KYBAL, Vlastimil, 1935: *Po československých stopách v Latinské Americe*. Prague: Česká akademie věd a umění, 90 pp.

339 NÁLEVKA, V., 1968: 'Slovanský kongres v Montevideu. (Příspěvek k dějinám československého krajanského hnutí v Latinské Americe za druhé světové války)', *RDS*, no. 5, pp. 709-729.

340 NÁLEVKA, V., 1971: 'El consorcio de Bata en América Latina durante la segunda guerra mundial', *IAP*, yr. 5, pp. 183-191.

341 NÁLEVKA, V., 1975: 'Los congresos eslavos de Buenos Aires y Montevideo en la Segunda Guerra Mundial', *IAP*, yr. 9, pp. 107-121.

342 POLIŠENSKÝ, Josef, 1976: 'La emigración checoslovaca a América Latina, 1649-1945. Problemas y fuentes', *JGSWGL*, vol. 13, pp. 56-72.

343 POLIŠENSKÝ, Josef, 1986: 'Problems of studying the history of Czech mass emigration to the Americas', in *Emigration from northern, central and southern Europe: theoretical and methodological principles of research.* Cracow, pp. 185-194.

344 VASILIJEV, I., 1986: 'Vystěhovalectví Cechů a Slováků do Latinské Ameriky před druhou světovou válkou', *CL*, 73/4, pp. 239-243.

Argentina

345 BAĎURA, B., 1981: 'K historii prvních spolků českých a slovenských vystěhovalců v Argentině. Sborník k problematice dějin imperialismu', in *Sborník k problematice dějin imperialismu.* Prague: Ústav českosloven-ských a světových dějin, *ČSAV*, no. 11, pp. 279-332.

346 DUBOVICKÝ, Ivan, 1987: 'Krajanská kolonie Presidencia Roque Saenz

Peña (Příspěvek k počátkům českého vystěhovalectví do Argentiny)', *CC*, no. 2, pp. 139-181.

347   DUBOVICKÝ, Ivan, 1988: 'La política emigratoria en Bohemia en relación con Argentina, 1848-1938', *IAP*, yr. 22.

348   DUBOVICKÝ, Ivan, 1988: 'Kolonizační pokusy v Argentině a meziválečná Československá republika', *CC*, no. 3, pp. 193-236.

349   DUBOVICKÝ, Ivan, 1989: 'Formování českého a slovenského etnika v Argentině', *CC*, no. 4, pp. 130-141.

350   DUFOUR, Jorge A., 1981: 'Presencia de los checoslovacos en la colonización del Chaco', in *Actas del II Encuentro de Geohistoria Regional*. Posadas.

351   KAPITOLA, L., 1980: 'K historii slovenské emigracě v Argentině', *SZ*, no. 6, pp. 28-43.

352   MÍŠEK, Rudolf, 1967: 'Origen de la emigración checoslovaca a la Argentina', *IAP*, yr. 1, pp. 123-131.

See also: 341

Brazil

353   BARTEČEK, Ivo, 1987: 'A emigração checa e eslovaca para o Brasil no período entre duas guerras mundiais', *IAP*, yr. 21.

354   BARTEČEK, Ivo, 1988: 'Československá kolonizace v Brazílii', *CC*, no. 3, pp. 237-251.

355   MOUT, Nicolette, 1969: 'Os primeros Tchecos no Brasil', *IAP*, yr. 3, pp. 219-223.

Cuba

356   NÁLEVKA, Vladimír, 1970: 'La colonia checoslovaca en Cuba durante la segunda Guerra Mundial', *IAP*, yr. 4, pp. 231-235.

Uruguay

See: 341

DANISH

General

357   ANDERSEN, Winni, Charlotte EGEBLAD and Helle THERKILDSEN, 1986: 'Dansk udvandringsstruktur i 1920 erne', *EM*, no. 2, pp. 12-21.

358   ESSINGER, Bent E., 1979: 'La emigración danesa', in *La emigración europea a la América Latina: fuentes y estado de investigación (informes presentados a la IV Reunión de Historiadores Latinoamericanistas Europeos)*. Berlin: Colloquium Verlag (Bibliotheca Ibero-Americana), pp. 85-99.

See also: 1386; 1387

Argentina

359   BJERG. Maria M., 1989: 'Identidad étnica y solidaridad en un grupo migratorio minoritario: un análisis de la "Sociedad Danesa de Socorros Mutuos", 1892-1930', *EML*, no. 12, pp. 383-404.

360   JENSEN, Janni and Peter DYBDAL LARSEN, 1988: *Den danske Argentinaudvandring fra midten af det 19. århundrede til mellemkrigstiden: dens forløb og særtræk*. Aalborg: Speciale i historie fra AUC, 135 pp.

361   KOHN LONCARICA, Alfredo G., 1984: 'La inmigración médica escandinava en la Argentina', *HA*, no. 13, pp. 73-84.

362   LILLEØR, Niels Carl, 1987: *Blandt Gauchoer og Godtfolk: Rejse i danskernes Argentina*. Odense: Odense Universitetsforlag, 122 pp.

Brazil

363   ERIKSEN, Gert and Steen OUSAGER, 1981: *Med æselspark og piper cub i Minas Gerais: en dansk mejerisucces i det indre Brasilien*. São Paulo: Fundo Dinamarca, 86 pp.

364   OTTE, Helle, 1988: *Danske erhvervsimmigranter i Brasilien*. Aalborg: Udvandrerarkivet (Udvandrerhistoriske studier nr. 2), 71 pp.

Venezuela

365   OTTE, Helle and Paul Erik OLSEN, 1986: 'Udvandring med statsgaranti? - om det danske kolonisationsforsøg i Venezuela 1938', *EM*, no. 2, pp. 22-33.

DUTCH

Argentina

366 JONGKIND, C.F., 1985: 'The Dutch colony in Tres Arroyos, Argentina: a particular case of ethnic group maintenance', *IM*, 23/3, pp. 335-347.

367 JONGKIND, C.F., 1986: 'Ethnic solidarity and social stratification: migrants' organizations in Peru and Argentina', *BELC*, no. 40, pp. 37-48.

See also: 40

Brazil

368 ABREU, Adilson Avansi de, 1971: *A colonização agrícola holandesa do estado de São Paulo*. Holambra I. São Paulo: Universidade de São Paulo (Instituto de Geografia, Série Teses e Monografias, no. 6), 114 pp.

369 AUGELLI, J., 1958: 'A Dutch colony in Brazil', *GR*, vol. 58, pp. 431-3.

370 BOSCH, F., 1983: *Arapoti: een Hollandse boer in Brazilië vertelt*. Arapoti.

371 BRONKHORST, N.A., 1985: *25 Jaar Arapoti: 1960-1985*. [Arapoti]: Bronkhorst, 145 pp.

372 BUYSSE, Frans, 1984: *Zeeuwse gemeenschap van Holambra, Brazilië (1858-1982): een antropologische studie over integratie en identiteit*. Aardenburg: Heemkundige Kring West-Zeeuws-Vlaanderen (Bijdragen tot de geschiedenis van West-Zeeuws-Vlaanderen, nr. 13), 152 pp.

373 CORTES, G. de Menezes, 1957: 'Colonie hollandaise au Brésil: Holambra, organisation, enseignements', *PN*, 12/2, pp. 269-288.

374 GASSELTE, Klaas van, 1989: *Fazenda van Castrolanda: over boeren en boerinnen die hun tenten opsloegen op de campo's van Brazilië*. Bedum: Profiel, 283 pp.

375 GIER, P.J. de, 1990: *Nederlandse emigranten in Brazilië*. Lelystad: Stichting IVIO (Actuele Onderwerpen, no. 2312), 20 pp.

376 HACK, Hendrik, 1959: *Dutch group settlement in Brazil*. Amsterdam: Royal Tropical Institute (Department of Cultural and Physical Anthropol-

ogy), 67 pp.

377   JONGKIND, C.F., 1986: 'Nederlandse boerengemeenschappen in Paraná, Brazilië: Deel 1: Carambei, een succesvolle vestiging van Nederlandse immigranten', *EPE*, no. 4, pp. 6-20.

378   JONGKIND, C.F., 1987: 'Nederlandse boerengemeenschappen in Paraná, Brazilië: Deel 2: Castrolanda, Arapotí en de centrale coöperatie (CCLPL)', *EPE*, no. 4, pp. 6-25.

379   JONGKIND, .C.F., 1989: 'The agrarian colonies of Dutch Calvinists in Paraná, Brazil', *IM*, 27/3, pp. 497-485.

380   KOOY, Hendrik Adrianus, 1986: *Carambei 75 jaar: 1911-1986*. [Carambei]: [H.A. Kooy], 291 pp.

381   LHOEST, G.L.M., 1988: *Nederlandse migrant als ontwikkelingswerker: brengen de Nederlandse agrarische nederzettingen in Brazilië ontwikkeling in het gebied waarin ze gevestigd zijn?*. [Tilburg]: [Lhoest], 123 pp.

382   LOS, D., 1959: *Dutch group settlement in Brazil*. The Hague.

383   LUYTEN, Sonia Maria Bibe, 1981: 'Der Beitrag Kommunikationsmittel zur Akkulturation der Holländer in Paraná', *SJ*, vol. 29, pp. 107-116.

384   LUYTEN, Sonia Maria Bibe, 1981: *Comunicação e aculturação: a colonização holondesa no Paraná*. São Paulo: Edições Loyola (Serie comunicação, no. 22), 152 pp.

385   LUYTEN, Sonia Maria Bibe, 1986: 'Holandeses no Brasil e nos Estados Unidos. Uma visão comparativa', *RA*, vol. 29, pp. 73-84.

386   MEER, K. van der, 1961: *50 anos Carambei: como crescue a colonia*. Franeker: Wever, 47 pp.

387   RIJK-ZAAT, Elly de, ed., 1990: *Toen wij uit Nederland vertrokken ... : Ervaringen van Nederlandse emigranten op kolonies in Brazilië*. 's-Gravenhage: Katholieke Vereniging van Ouders en Familieleden van Geëmigreerden, 48 pp.

388   SALDANHA, P., 1960: 'Estudo genético e antropológico de uma colônia de holondeses do Brasil', *RA*, 8/1, pp. 1-42.

389   SANTEN, Cornelius Marius Petrus van, 1966: 'Die holländischen Bauernsiedlungen in Brasilien', *SJ*, vol. 14, pp. 103-120.

390   SMITS, Mari, 1990: *Holambra: Geschiedenis van een Nederlandse*

toekomstdroom in de Braziliaanse werkelijkheid 1948-1988. Nijmegen: Katholiek Documentatie Centrum (Werkschriften van het Katholiek Documentatie Centrum voor de geschiedschrijving van het Nederlands katholicisme, no. 2), 211 pp.

391   STRAATEN, Harald S. van der, 1988: *Hollandse pioniers in Brazilië*. Franeker: Uitgeverij Van Wijnen, 160 pp.

392   WIJNEN, C.J.M., 1976: *Holambra I: Nederlandse boeren in coöperatief verband in Brazilië*. Den Haag: Landbouw-Economisch Instituut (Mededelingen, no. 138), 88 pp.

393   WIJNEN, C.J.M., 1977: *Holambra II: een groepsvestiging van Nederlandse boeren in Brazilië*. Den Haag: Landbouw-Economisch Instituut (Mededelingen, no. 178), 81 pp.

Chile

394   QUIROZ LARREA, Daniel, 1984: 'La colonia "Nueva Transvaal" de Gorbea: colonización extranjera en la Araucanía', *BMRA*, no. 1, pp. 25-39.

395   QUIROZ LARREA, Daniel, 1985: 'La colonia "Nueva Transvaal" de Gorbea: documentos y noticias (1901-1903)', *BMRA*, no. 2, pp. 11-23.

396   QUIROZ LARREA, Daniel, 1985: 'Colonos holandeses en la Araucanía: Klaas de Groot Rietwink (1878-1953)', *BMRA*, no. 2, pp. 135-140.

FINNISH
(including Swedish-Finns)

Bibliography

397 KOIVUKANGAS, Olavi and Simo TOIVONEN, 1978: *Suomen siirtolaisuuden ja maassamuuton. A bibliography on Finnish emigration and internal migration.* Turku: Siirtolaisuusintituutti, 226 pp.

General

398 KORKIASAARI, Jouni, 1989: *Suomalaiset maailmalla: suomen siirtolaisuus ja ulkosuomalaiset entisajoista tähän päivään.* Turku: Siirtolaisuusinstituutti, 161 pp.

399 LÄHTEENMÄKI, Olavi, 1979: 'La emigración finlandesa', in *La emigración europea a la América Latina: fuentes y estado de investigación (informes presentados a la IV Reunión de Historiadores Latinoamericanistas Europeos).* Berlin: Colloquium Verlag (Bibliotheca Ibero-Americana), pp. 100-103.

400 LÄHTEENMÄKI, Olavi, 1981: 'Finnish group immigration to Latin America', in Michael G. Karni, ed., *Finnish diaspora*, vol. I. Toronto: The Multicultural History Society of Ontario, pp. 289-301.

401 LÄHTEENMÄKI, Olavi, n.d: 'Paratiisin etsintää ja pettyyksiä – siirtolaiskirjeitä Etelä-Amerikasta-Suomeen', in Eero Kuparinen, ed., *Maitten ja merten takaa.* Helsinki, pp. 136-155.

Argentina

402 LÄHTEENMÄKI, Olavi, 1989: *Colonia Finlandesa. Uuden Suomen perustaminen Argentiinaan 1900-luvun alussa* (ed. by Reino Kero with summary in English). Vammala: Historical Society of Finland (Historiallisia Tutkimuksia, nr. 154), 282 pp.

403 PÄRSSINEN, Ilkka, 1974: 'Argentiinan ja Paraguayn Suomaisetasiirtokunnat', *SM*, no. 1, pp. 27-32.

404 SCHLUETER, Regina G., 1984: *Finlandeses en la Argentina.* Buenos Aires: Centro de Investigaciones en Turismo, 33 pp.

405 TESSIERI, Enrique, 1979: 'The second generation Finns of Argentina: a

process towards Argentinization', *SM*, no. 2, pp. 8-14.

406   TESSIERI, Enrique and KAUKAINEN, Maani, 1986:   *Päätepysäkki Colonia Finlandesa*. Juva, 236 pp.

Brazil

407   AHVENAINEN-SALIN, Betty, 1966:   *Betty, Donna Bettynä Brasiliassa*. Porvoo, 188 pp.

408   HILDEN, Eva, 1989:   *A saga de Penedo: a história da colônia finlandesa no Brasil*. Rio de Janeiro, 111 pp.

409   LÄHTEENMÄKI, Olavi, 1979:   'Viisi peninkulmaa Penedon taivalta. Brasilian suomalainen siirtolaine Fazenda Penedo 1929-1979', *SI*, no. 1, pp. 29-42.

410   PENNANEN, H.D., 1929:   *Fazenda Penedo, Suomalainen maanviljelystila Brasiliassa*. Tampere, 32 pp.

411   UUSKALLIO, Toivo, 1929:   *Matkalla kohti tropiikin taikaa (Fazenda Penedoa)*. Helsinki, 128 pp.

Cuba

412   JARVA, Ritva, 1971:   *Cuba – 'paradise' for Finns*. Turku: University of Turku (Institute of General History, Publication No. 3), 16 pp.

Dominican Republic

413   LÄHTEENMÄKI, Olavi, 1980:   'Dominikaanisen tasavallan suomalainen viljavakka', *SM*, no. 4, pp. 21-32.

FRENCH

Bibliography

414   MAURO, Frédéric, 1983: 'Capitales, empresarios y obreros franceses en los procesos de industrialización y sindicalización de América Latina', in *Capitales, empresarios y obreros europeos en América Latina (Actas del 6° Congreso de AHILA, Stockholm, 25-28 de Mayo 1981)*. Stockholm: Instituto de Estudios Latinoamericanos (monografías, no. 8, vol. 1), pp. 31-76.

General

415   LAYBOURN, Norman, 1986: *L'émigration des alsaciens et des lorrains du XVIIIe au XXe siècle: essai d'histoire démographique*, vol. II. Strasbourg: Association des Publications près les Universités de Strasbourg, 501 pp.

416   MAURO, Frédéric, 1979: 'La emigración francesa a la América Latina. Fuentes y estado de investigación', in *La emigración europea a la América Latina: fuentes y estado de investigación (informes presentados a la IV Reunión de Historiadores Latinoamericanistas Europeos)*. Berlin: Colloquium Verlag (Bibliotheca Ibero-Americana), pp. 153-164.

Argentina

417   ÁLVAREZ, Gregorio, 1961: 'La primera colonia francesa del Neuquén', *RSAEF*, no. extraord., pp. 31-37.

418   ANDREU, Jean, et al, 1977: *Les Aveyronnais dans la Pampa: fondation, développement et vie de la colonie aveyronnaise de Pigüé, Argentine, 1884-1974*. Toulouse: Edonard Privat, 325 pp.

419   BENNASAR, Bartolomé, 1976: 'La inmigración francesa a la Argentina a finales del siglo XIX: el caso de la colonia Pigüé y el problema de las fuentes', *JGSWGL*, vol. 13, pp. 174-180.

420   CABANETTES, Emile and Pierre GOMBERT, 1988: *Pigüe: ces français devenus "gauchos"*. Rodez: Editions du Rouergue, 219 pp.

421   CHARVET, J.P. and V. REY, 1980: 'La migration des agriculteurs outre-atlantique, fait anecdotique, ou socio-économique?', *ECR*, no. 135, pp. 44-49.

422 GAIGNARD, Romain, 1968: 'La faillité de l'expérience de colonisation agricole des "Pieds-Noirs" en Argentine', *COM*, vol. 21, pp. 308-317.

423 GUZMÁN DE TOSCANO, Nedy Beatriz, 1978: *Estancias de Azul y pobladores franceses en la zona rural de Azul*. La Plata: Instituto San Vicente de Paul, 222 pp.

424 OTERO, Hernán, 1990: 'Una visión crítica da la endogamia: reflexiones a partir de una reconstrucción de familias francesas (Tandil, 1850-1914)', *EML*, no. 15-16, pp. 343-378.

425 SZUCHMAN, Mark D., 1980: 'La colonia francesa en la ciudad de Córdoba. La "Société Française de Secours Mutuels"', *RH*, no. 6, pp. 207-217.

426 ZAGO, Manrique, ed., 1986: *Los franceses en la Argentina - Les Français en Argentine*. Buenos Aires: Manrique Zago Ediciones, 191 pp.

Brazil

427 EISENBERG-BACH, Susan, 1983: 'French and German writers in exile in Brazil: reception and translation', in Hans-Bernhard Moeller, ed., *Latin America and the literature of exile*. Heidelberg: Carl Winter Universität-sverlag, pp. 293-307.

428 NOGUEIRA, Emilia, 1953: 'Alguns aspectos da influência francêsa em São Paulo na segunda metade do século XIX', *RH/SP* 7/4, pp. 317-342.

429 TAUNAY, Affonso d'Escragnolle, 1956: *A missão artística de 1816*. Rio de Janeiro: D.P.H.A.N. and São Paulo: Revista dos Tribunais, 351 pp.

Chile

430 ROUDIE, P. ed., 1987: *Un Français au Chili, 1841-1853. Correspondance et notes de voyage de Joseph Miran*. Paris: Centre National de la Recherche Scientifique (Maison des Pays Ibériques), 161 pp.

Cuba

431 DUHARTE JIMÉNEZ, Rafael, 1987: 'La huella de la emigración francesa en Santiago de Cuba', *DC*, no. 10.

432 LUX, William R., 1972: 'French colonization in Cuba, 1791-1809', *AM*, 29/1, pp. 57-61.

Mexico

433   GOUY, P., 1980: *Pérégrinations des "Barcelonnettes" au Mexique*. Grenoble: Presse Universitaire de Grenoble, 159 pp.

434   MEYER, Jean A., 1974: 'Les français au Mexique au XIXème siècle', *CAL*, vol. 9/10, pp. 43-86.

435   PROAL, Maurice and Pierre M. CHARPENEL, 1986: *L'empire des Barcelonnettes au Mexique*. Marseille: Editions J. Laffitte, 127 pp.

Paraguay

436   CHOAY, Corinne, 1977: 'L'échec d'une colonisation française au Paraguay au milieu du XIX siècle', *CAL*, no. 16, pp. 31-50.

437   PITAUD, Henri, 1955: *Les français au Paraguay*. Bordeaux: Editions Bière, 224 pp.

Puerto Rico

438   CAMUÑAS MADERA, Ricardo R., 1989: 'Los franceses en el oeste de Puerto Rico', *CV*, no. 53, pp. 25-36.

439   LUQUE DE SÁNCHEZ, María Dolores, 1982: *La inmigración corsa a Puerto Rico durante el siglo XIX*. San Juan: Alianza Francesa.

440   LUQUE DE SÁNCHEZ, María Dolores, 1987-8: 'Con pasaporte francés en el Puerto Rico del siglo XIX (1778-1850)', *BCIH*, no. 3, pp. 95-122.

441   PASSALACQUA, John Luis Antonio, 'La inmigración corsa al partido de Coamo hacia fines del siglo XVIII y principios del siglo XIX', *RH/SJu*, no. 3, pp. 97-138.

Uruguay

442   DUPREY, Jacques, 1952: *Voyage aux origines françaises de l'Uruguay*. Montevideo: Instituto Histórico y Geográfico del Uruguay.

443   MARENALES ROSSI, Martha and Guy BOURDÉ, 1977: 'L'immigration française et le peuplement de l'Uruguay, 1830-1860', *CAL*, no. 16, pp. 7-30.

444   MORGAN, Iwan, 1983: 'Orleanist diplomacy and the French colony in Uruguay', *IHR*, 5/2, pp. 201-28.

Venezuela

445 SANZ TAPIA, Angel, 1987: 'Refugiados de la Revolución Francesa en Venezuela (1793-1795)', *RI*, 47/181, pp. 833-867.

446 VERNA, Paul, 1979: 'Les français dans l'histoire du Vénézuela', *CV*, no. 32.

GERMAN

General

447   BLANCPAIN, Jean-Pierre, 1988: 'Origines et caractères des migrations germaniques en Amérique Latine au XIXe siècle', *JGSWGL*, vol. 25, pp. 349-383.

448   BLANCPAIN, Jean-Pierre, 1989: 'Des visées pangermanistes au noyautage hitlérien. Le nationalisme allemand et l'Amérique latine (1890-1945)', *RHI*, no. 570, pp. 433-482.

449   BOPP, Marianne O. de, 1973: 'Die Exilsituation in Mexiko', in Manfred Durzak, ed., *Die deutsche Exilliteratur 1933-1945*. Stuttgart: Reclam, pp. 175-182.

450   CAEIRO, Oscar, 1983: 'Profile of German and Spanish exile poets in Latin America', in Hans-Bernhard Moeller, ed., *Latin America and the literature of exile*. Heidelberg: Carl Winter Universitätsverlag, pp. 181-206

451   GÜENAGA DE SILVA, Rosario, 1989: 'La presencia alemana en el extremo austral de América', *JGSWGL*, vol. 26, pp. 201-228.

452   ILG, Karl, 1976: *Pioniere in Argentinien, Chile, Paraguay und Venezuela. Durch Bergwelt, Urwald und Steppe erwanderte Volkskunde der deutschsprachigen Siedler*. Innsbruck and Vienna: Tyrolia Verlag, 318 pp.

453   KELLENBENZ, Hermann and Jürgen SCHNEIDER, 1976: 'La emigración alemana a América Latina desde 1821 hasta 1930', *JGSWGL*, vol. 13, pp. 386-403.

454   KELLENBENZ, Hermann and Jürgen SCHNEIDER, 1979: 'La emigración alemana para América Latina (1815-1929/31). Fuentes y estado de investigación', in *La emigración europea a la América Latina: fuentes y estado de investigación*. Berlin: Colloquium Verlag (Biblioteca Ibero--Americana), pp. 179-194.

455   KIEBLING, Wolfgang, 1981: *Kunst und Literatur im antifaschistischen Exil 1933-1945: Exil in Lateinamerika*. Frankfurt: Röderberg, 578 pp.

456   LUDWIG, Walther, 1990: 'Ein deutscher Kaufmann in Südamerika, 1905-1911', *JGSWGL*, vol. 27, pp. 337-374.

457   NEWTON, Ronald C., 1983: 'Das andere Deutschland: the anti-fascist exile

network in southern South America', in Jarrell C. Jackman and Carla M. Borden, eds., *The muses flee Hitler: cultural transfer and adaptation 1930-1945*. Washington, D.C.: Smithsonian Institute Press, pp. 303-314.

458   POHLE, Fritz, 1989: *Emigrationstheater in Südamerika*. Hamburg: Hamburger Arbeitsstelle für deutsche Exilliteratur (Schriftenreihe des P. Walter Jacob-Archivs Nr. 2), 101 pp.

459   POMMERIN, Reiner, 1979: 'Überlegungen des "Dritten Reichs" zur Rückholung deutscher Auswanderer aus Lateinamerika', *JGSWGL*, vol. 16, pp. 365-378.

460   PRIEN, Hans, J., 1986: 'Kirchengeschichte Lateinamerikas. Ein Forschungsbericht', *TL*, no. 111, pp. 785-799.

461   SPALEK, John M., 1983: 'The varieties of exile experience: German, Polish and Spanish writers', in Hans-Bernhard Moeller, ed., *Latin America and the literature of exile*. Heidelberg: Carl Winter Universitätsverlag, pp. 71-90.

462   WALKER, Mack, 1964: *Germany and the emigration, 1816-1885*. Cambridge, Mass.: Harvard University Press, 284 pp.

463   ZUR MUEHLEN, Patrik von, 1988: *Fluchtziel Lateinamerika. Die deutsche Emigration 1933-1945: politische Aktivitäten und sozio-kulturelle Integration.* Bonn: Verlag Neue Gesellschaft, 335 pp.

See also: 198; 200; 865; 867; 868

Central America

464   FRÖSCHLE, Hartmut, 1979: 'Die Deutschen in Mittelamerika', in Hartmut Fröschle, ed., *Die Deutschen in Lateinamerika*. Tübingen and Basle: Horst Erdmann Verlag, pp. 565-576.

465   SCHOONOVER, Thomas D., 1988: 'Germany in Central America, 1820s to 1929: an overview', *JGSWGL*, vol. 25, pp. 33-59.

Argentina

466   BOSCH, Beatriz, 1977: 'La colonización de los alemanes del Volga en Entre Ríos, 1878-1888', *IE*, no. 23, pp. 295-310.

467   CIAPPA, Frederico Carlos, 1987: 'La "colonia científica" alemana en La Plata, 1906-1945', *TH*, 21/244, pp. 34-45.

468   GRAEFE, Iris Barbara, 1971: *Zur Volkskunde der Rußlanddeutschen in Argentinien*. Vienna: Verlag A. Schendl, 162 pp.

469   GÜENAGA DE SILVA, Rosario, 1989: 'La presencia alemana en el extremo austral de América', *JGSWGL*, vol. 26, pp. 201-227.

470   HAYDEE HIPPERDINGER, Yolanda, 1990: 'Las colonias alemanas del Volga de Coronel Suárez: mantenimiento lingüístico', *EML*, no. 15-16, pp. 407-424.

471   HOFFMANN, Werner, 1979: 'Die Deutschen in Argentinien', in Hartmut Fröschle, ed., *Die Deutschen in Lateinamerika*. Tübingen and Basle: Horst Erdmann Verlag, pp. 40-145.

472   JACKISCHE, Carlota, 1987: 'Los refugiados alemanos en la Argentina', *TH*, 21/244, pp. 6-33.

473   JACKISCHE, Carlota, 1989: *El Nazismo y los refugiados alemanes en la Argentina 1933-1945*. Buenos Aires: Editorial de Belgrano, 306 pp.

474   KLOBERDANZ, Timothy J., 1980: 'Plainsmen of three continents: Volga German adaptation to steppe, prairie, and pampa', in Frederick C. Luebke, ed., *Ethnicity on the Great Plains*. Lincoln: University of Nebraska Press, pp. 54-72.

475   KOPP, Thomas, 1979: *Wolgadeutsche Siedeln im Argentinischen Zwischen-stromland*. Marburg: N. G. Elwert, 287 pp.

476   MICOLIS, Marisa, 1973: *Une communauté allemande en Argentine: Eldorado*. Québec: Centre International de Recherche sur le Bilinguisme (Publication B-41), 208 pp.

477   NEWTON, R.C., 1976: 'Social change, cultural crisis and the origins of Nazism within the German speaking community of Buenos Aires', *NS*, 1/2, pp. 395-420.

478   NEWTON, Ronald C., 1977: *German Buenos Aires, 1900-1933: social change and social crisis*. Austin: University of Texas Press, 225 pp.

479   NEWTON, Ronald C., 1981: 'The German-Argentines between Nazism and nationalism: the Patagonia Plot of 1939', *IHR*, 3/1, pp. 77-114.

480   NEWTON, Ronald C., 1982: 'Indifferent sanctuary: German-speaking refugees and exiles in Argentina, 1933-1945', *JIASWA*, 24/4, pp. 395-420.

481   NEWTON, Ronald C., 1984: 'The United States, the German Argentines and the myth of the Fourth Reich, 1943-47', *HAHR*, vol. 64, pp. 81-103.

482   NEWTON, Ronald C., 1988: 'Los Estados Unidos, los germano-argentinos y el mito del Cuarto Reich 1943-1947', *RHA*, no. 105, pp. 111-146.

483   OCKIER, Maria Cristina, 1988: 'Inmigrantes y élites en la distribución de la tierra de la "Colonia Roca" (Río Negro)', *AN*, segunda época, no. 13, pp. 301-341.

484   PYENSON, Lewis, 1985: *Cultural imperialism and exact sciences: German expansion overseas 1900-1930.* New York: Peter Lang, 342 pp.

485   ROJER, Olga Elaine, 1989: *Exile in Argentina, 1933-1945: a historical and literary introduction.* New York: Peter Lang New York, 250 pp.

486   SEEFELD, Ruth, 1985: 'La emigración alemana y la inmigración alemana en la Argentina', in *La Inmigración a América Latina (primeras Jornadas internacionales sobre la migración en América).* México, DF: Instituto Panamericano de Geografía e Historia (Serie inmigración, tomo 2), pp. 135-152.

487   SUTIN, Stewart Edward, 1975: *The impact of Nazism on the Germans of Argentina.* PhD Thesis, University of Texas, Austin.

488   SUTIN, Stewart Edward, 1976: *The Germans of Misiones.* New York: Center for Latin American and Caribbean Studies, New York University (Occasional Papers no. 23), 20 pp.

489   VALLA, Celso José, 1978: *Las alemanes del Volga y los Salesianos en la Pampa.* La Plata, 83 pp.

490   VOLBERG, Heinrich, 1981: *Auslandsdeutschtum und Drittes Reich. Der Fall Argentinien.* Cologne and Vienna: Bölau Verlag, 221 pp.

491   WEYNE, Olga, 1984: 'Inmigrantes alemanes del Volga en la Argentina', *SE*, 21/74, pp. 208-228.

492   WEYNE, Olga, 1987: *El último puerto. Del Rhin al Volga y del Volga al Plata.* Buenos Aires: Instituto Torcuato Di Tella, 305 pp.

493   ZAGO, Manrique, ed., 1985: *Presencia alemana y austriaca en la Argentina – Deutsche und österreichische Präsenz in Argentinien.* Buenos Aires: Manrique Zago Ediciones, 220 pp.

See also: 71; 452; 879; 880; 909

Belize

494   ROBINSON, St.John, 1985: 'German migration to Belize: the beginnings', *BS*, 13/3-4, pp. 17-40.

Bolivia

495   CRESPO, Alberto, 1978: *Alemanes en Bolivia*. La Paz: Editorial los Amigos del Libro, 247 pp.

496   FRÖSCHLE, Hartmut and Reinhard WOLFF, 1979: 'Die Deutschen in Bolivien', in Hartmut Fröschle, ed., *Die Deutschen in Lateinamerika*. Tübingen and Basle: Horst Erdmann Verlag, pp. 146-168.

497   OSTERWEIL, Marc Jeffrey, 1978: *The meaning of elitehood: Germans, Jews and Arabs in La Paz, Bolivia*. PhD Thesis, New York University.

Brazil

498   AMADO, Janaina, 1978: *Conflito social no Brasil: a revolta dos 'Mucker'*. Rio Grande do Sul, 1868-1898. São Paulo: Editora Símbolo, 303 pp.

499   ANUSZEWSKA, Ewa, 1980: 'A imigração alemã no Brasil à luz dos relatórios dos cônsules do Império Alemão no início do século XX', *EL*, no. 7, pp. 51-66.

500   BALHANA, Altiva Pilatti and Cecilia Maria WESTPHALEN, 1983: 'Os alemães no comércio e na indústria do Paraná 1890-1929', in *Capitales, empresarios y obreros europeos en América Latina (Actas del 6° Congreso de AHILA, Stockholm, 25-28 de Mayo 1981)*. Stockholm: Instituto de Estudios Latinoamericanos (monografías no. 8, vol. 2), pp. 383-405.

501   BECKER, Itala Irene Basile, 1976: 'O índio Kaingang e a colonização alemã', in *Anais do II simpósio de história da imigração e colonização alemã no Rio Grande do Sul*. São Leopoldo, pp. 45-72.

502   BIRKHEAD, Ceres Boeira, 1987: 'Constructing a home in the New World: the immigrants' experience as reflected in German-Brazilian almanacs and newspapers, 1850-1930', in *Seminar on the acquisition of Latin American Library Materials (Papers of the thirty-first annual meeting, University of Wisconsin. Madison)*. Madison, pp. 69-80.

503   CARNEIRO, Daví, 1963/4: 'Deutsche Mitarbeit in Paraná, vornehmlich im 19. Jahrhundert', *SJ*, vols. 11-12, pp. 169-180.

504 DESAULNIERS, Julieta Beatriz, 1986: 'Colono alemão: abandonado ou explorado?', *EIA*, 12/2, pp. 73-103.

505 DREHER, Martin, 1984: *Igreja e Germanidade*. Porto Alegre: Escola Superior de Teologia and São Leopoldo: Editora Sinodal.

506 CARAVALHO, Tania Franco, 1987: 'A imigração alemã e o romance no Sul do Brasil', *BEPB*, no. 46-47, pp. 185-197.

507 DALBY, Richard Overton, 1969: *The German private schools of southern Brazil during the Vargas years, 1930-1945: German nationalism vs. Brazilian nationalization*. PhD Thesis, Indiana University.

508 FAUSEL, Erich, 1959: *Die deutschbrasilianische Sprachmischung. Probleme, Vorgang und Wortbestand*. Berlin: Erich Schmidt Verlag, 230 pp.

509 FISCHER, Joachim, 1967: 'Der Kampf gegen die Pseudopfarrer in Rio Grande do Sul im 19. Jahrhundert', *DED*, 38, pp. 94-118.

510 GAPPMAIER, Josef, 1979/80: 'Bericht über die Entwicklung der Donauschwabensiedlung Entre Rios bei Guarapuava, Paraná, Brasilien', *SJ*, 27-28, pp. 51-59.

511 GERTZ, René, 1987: *O fascismo no sul do Brasil: germanismo, nazismo, integralismo*. Porto Alegre: Mercado Aberto, 205 pp.

512 GLADE, James J., 1979: 'Nordic farmers and Latin cattle barons: problems faced by German settlers in southern Brazil', *RHA*, no. 87, pp. 127-139.

513 GROVER, Mark L., 1989: 'The Mormon Church and German immigrants in southern Brazil: religion and language', *JGSWGL*, vol. 26, pp. 295-308.

514 HARMS-BALTZER, Käte, 1970: *Die Nationalisierung der deutschen Einwanderer und ihrer Nachkommen in Brasilien als Problem der deutsch--brasilianischen Beziehungen 1930-1938*. Berlin: Colloquium Verlag (Bibliotheca Ibero-Americana), 244 pp.

515 HILTON, Stanley E., 1981: *Hitler's secret war in South America, 1939-1945*. Baton Rouge: Louisiana State University Press, 353 pp.

516 ILG, Karl, 1978: *Das Deutschtum in Brasilien*. Vienna: Schutzverein "Oster Landsmannschaft", 103 pp.

517 ILG, Karl and Karl H. OBERACKER, 1979: 'Die Deutschen in Brasilien', in Hartmut Fröschle, ed., *Die Deutschen in Lateinamerika*. Tübingen and Basle: Horst Erdmann Verlag, pp. 169-300.

518   JORDAN, T.G., 1962: 'Aspects of German colonization in southern Brazil', *SSSQ*.

519   KELLENBENZ, Hermann and Jürgen SCHNEIDER, 1980: 'A imagem do Brasil na Alemanha do século XIX: impressões e estereótipos da independencia ao fim da monarquia', *EL*, no. 6, pt. 2, pp. 71-101.

520   KLUCK, Patricia Ann, 1975: *Decision making among descendants of German immigrant farmers in Rio Grande do Sul.* PhD Thesis, Cornell University.

521   LANDO, Aldair Marli and Eliane CRUXÊN BARROS, 1976: *A colonização alemã no Rio Grande do Sul: uma interpretação sociológica.* Porto Alegre: Editora Movimento, 94 pp.

522   LUEBKE, Frederick C., 1983: 'The German ethnic group in Brazil: the ordeal of World War I', *YGAS*, vol. 18, pp. 255-267.

523   LUEBKE, Frederick C., 1983: 'A prelude to conflict: the German ethnic group in Brazilian society, 1890-1917', *ERS*, vol. 6, pp. 1-17.

524   LUEBKE, Frederick C., 1987: *Germans in Brazil: a comparative history of cultural conflict during World War I.* Baton Rouge: Louisiana State University Press, 248 pp.

525   LUEBKE, Frederick C., 1990: *Germans in the New World.* Urbana and Chicago: University of Illinois Press, 198 pp.

526   MOEHLECKE, Germano Oscar, 1986: *Os imigrantes alemães e a Revolução Farroupilha.* São Leopoldo, 239 pp.

527   MULLER, K.D., 1974: *Pioneer settlement in south Brazil: the case of Toledo, Paraná.* The Hague: Martinus Nijhoff, 75 pp.

528   NICHOLS, Glenn A., and Philip S. SNYDER, 1981: 'Brazilian elites and the descendants of the German, Italian, and Japanese immigrants', *JIASWA*, 23/3, pp. 321-344.

529   OBERACKER Jr., Carlos H., 1965: 'Die Kolonie Riograndense (im Staate São Paulo) und ihre Nachbarkolonien im Jahre 1941', *JGSWGL*, vol. 2, pp. 373-398.

530   OBERACKER Jr., Carlos H., 1968: *A contribução teuta à formação da nação brasileira.* Rio de Janeiro: Editora Presença, 581 pp.

531   OBERACKER Jr., Carlos H., 1987: 'A colônia Leopoldina-Frankental na Bahia Meridional: una colônia européia de plantadores no Brasil', *JGSWGL*,

vol. 24, pp. 455-479.

532 OVERBECK, Wilhelm, 1923: *Fünfzig Jahre Deutscher Verein Germania und Deutschtum in Bahia*. Berlin: Druck von Emil Ebering, 200 pp.

533 PINSDORF, Marion K., 1989: *German-speaking entrepreneurs: builders of business in Brazil*. New York: Peter Lang, 366 pp.

534 PRIEN, Hans-Jürgen, 1988: 'Die "Deutsch-Evangelische Kirche" in Brasilien im Spannungsbogen von nationaler Wende (1933) und Kirchenkampf', *JGSWGL*, vol. 25, pp. 511-534.

535 PRIEN, Hans-Jürgen, 1989: *Evangelische Kirchwerdung in Brasilien: von den deutsch-evangelischen Einwanderergemeinden zur Evangelischen Kirche Lutherischen Bekenntnisses in Brasilien*. Gütersloh: Gütersloher Verlagshaus Gerd Mohn, 640 pp.

536 PRIEN, Hans-J.,1990: ' La Iglesia Germano-evangélica de Brasil entre el viraje nacional de 1933 y la Kirchenkampf', *EML*, no. 14, pp. 81-103.

537 RICHTER, Klaus, 1986: *A Sociedade Colonizadora Hanseática de 1897 e a colonização no interior de Joinville e Blumenau*. Florianópolis: Editora da Universidade Federal de Santa Catarina and Blumenau: Editora da Universidade Regional de Blumenau, 86 pp.

538 ROCHE, Jean, 1959: *La colonisation allemande et le Rio Grande do Sul*. Paris: Institut de Hautes Etudes de l'Amérique Latine, 696 pp.

539 ROCHE, Jean, 1965: 'Quelques aspects de la colonisation allemande en Espirito Santo', *CV*, no. 5, pp. 121-152.

540 ROCHE, Jean, 1968: *A colonização alemã no Espirito Santo*. São Paulo: Editora da Universidade de São Paulo, 367 pp.

541 SANT'ANA, Elma, 1985: *Jacobina Mauer*. Porto Alegre: Tchê!, 69 pp.

542 SEYFERTH, Giralda, 1974: *A colonização alemã no Vale do Itajai-Mirim*. Porto Alegre: Editôra Movimento, 159 pp.

543 SEYFERTH, Giralda, 1977: 'Identidade étnica numa comunidade teuto-brasileira do Vale do Itajaí', *RMP*, vol. 24, pp. 55-82.

544 SEYFERTH, Giralda, 1982: *Nacionalismo e identidade étnica: a ideologia germanista e o grupo étnico teuto-brasileiro numa comunidade do Vale do Itajai*. Florianópolis: Fundação Catarinense de Cultura, 223 pp.

545 SCHRAMM, Percy Ernst, 1964: 'Die deutsche Siedlungskolonie Dona

Francisca (Brasilien: St. Catharina) im Rahmen gleichzeitiger Projekte und Verhandlungen', *JGSWGL*, vol. 1, pp. 283-324.

546   STROBEL, Gustav Hermann, 1987: *Relatos de um pioneiro da imigração alemã*. Curitiba: Instituto Histórico, Geográfico e Etnográfico Paranaense (Estante Paranista 27), 142 pp.

547   VOLLWEILER, L.G., 1979: *Colonia Fritz: social adaptation of Danube Suabian pioneer farmers in a southern Brazilian frontier community*. PhD Thesis, University of Florida.

548   WAIBEL, Leo, 1955: *Die europäische Kolonisation in Südbrasilien*. Bonn: Ferd. Dümmlers Verlag.

549   WILLEMS, Emilio, 1940: *Assimilação e populações marginais no Brasil: estudo sociológico dos imigrantes Germânicos e seus descendentes*. São Paulo: Companhia Editora Nacional, 343 pp.

550   WILLEMS, Emilio, 1940: 'Assimilation of German immigrants in Brazil', *SSR*, 25/2, pp. 125-132.

551   WILLEMS, Emilio, 1942: 'Some aspects of cultural conflict and acculturation in southern rural Brazil', *RSO*, 7/4, pp. 375-84.

552   WILLEMS, Emilio, 1944: 'Acculturation and the horse complex among German Brazilians', *AA*, 46/2, pt. 1, pp. 153-161.

553   WILLEMS, Emilio, 1946: *A aculturação dos alemães no Brasil*. São Paulo: Editora Nacional, 609 pp.

See also: 192; 427; 602; 767; 949; 950; 956; 957; 958; 965; 969; 977

Chile

554   ABUFON LARACH, Juan, 1987: *Pequeña Alemania: análisis sociocultural de un enclave modernizador en Chile*. Santiago: Facultad de Filosofía, Humanidades y Educación, Universidad de Chile, 140 pp.

555   BLANCPAIN, Jean-Pierre, 1974: *Les Allemands au Chili (1816-1945)*. Cologne: Böhlau Verlag, 1162 pp.

556   CONVERSE, Christel, 1979: 'Die Deutschen in Chile', in Hartmut Fröschle, ed., *Die Deutschen in Lateinamerika*. Tübingen and Basle: Horst Erdmann Verlag, pp. 301-372.

557   ESTRADA, Baldomero, 1989: 'European expansion and regional

development: Valparaíso and German immigration in the second half of the XIX century', *ICM*, 7/1-2, pp. 7-22.

558   GAUDIG, Olaf and Peter VEIT, 1988: '¡...Y mañana el mundo entero! Antecedentes para la historia del nacional-socialismo en Chile', *ACH*, no. 41, pp. 99-117.

559   GEMBALLA, Gero, 1988: *Colonia Dignidad. Ein deutsches Lager in Chile*. Reinbek bei Hamburg: Rowohlt, 173 pp.

560   GOLTE, Winfried, 1973: *Das südchilenische Seengebiet; Besiedlung und wirtschaftliche Erschliessung seit dem 18. Jahrhundert*. Bonn: F. Dümmler in Kommission, 183 pp.

561   GUARDA, Gabriel, 1982: *Cartografía de la colonización alemana, 1846-1872*. Santiago: Ediciones Universidad Católica de Chile, 58 pp.

562   MARTINIC, Mateo, 1981: *Los alemanes en Magallanes*. Punta Arenas: Instituto de la Patagonia, 52 pp.

563   OJEDA EBERT, Gerardo Jorge, 1980: 'El rol de la inmigración alemana en el proceso de formación de la nación chilena', *EL*, no. 7, pp. 35-50.

564   OJEDA EBERT, Gerardo Jorge, 1983: 'Los dos polos de la presencia alemana en Chile y sus efectos (capitales alemanes e inmigración 1850-1918)', in *Capitales, empresarios y obreros europeos en América Latina (Actas del 6° Congreso de AHILA, Stockholm, 25-28 de Mayo 1981)*. Stockholm: Instituto de Estudios Latinoamericanos (monografías no. 8, vol. 2), pp. 600-616.

565   OJEDA EBERT, Gerardo Jorge, 1984: *Deutsche Einwanderung und Herausbildung der chilenischen Nation (1846-1920)*. Munich: Wilhem Fink Verlag, 216 pp.

566   SEDGEWICK, Ruth, 1949: 'German colonists in Chilean fiction', *HP*, 32/2, pp. 168-171.

567   WALDMANN, Peter, 1988: 'Conflicto cultural y adaptacion paulatina: la evolución de las colonias de inmigrantes alemanes en el sur de Chile', *JSWGL*, vol. 25, pp. 437-453.

568   YOUNG, George F.W., 1971: 'Bernardo Philippi, initiator of German colonization in Chile', *HAHR*, 51/3, pp. 478-496.

569   YOUNG, George F.W., 1974: *The Germans in Chile: immigration and colonization, 1849-1914*. New York: Center for Migration Studies, 234 pp.

See also: 452; 982

Colombia

570   ALLGAIER, Dieter, 1979: 'Die Deutschen in Kolumbien', in Hartmut Fröschle, ed., *Die Deutschen in Lateinamerika*. Tübingen and Basle: Horst Erdmann Verlag, pp. 433-474.

571   FRIEDE, Ivan, 1963: 'Colonos alemanes en la Sierra Nevada de Santa Marta', *RCA*, vol. 12, pp. 401-411.

572   KRAMER-KASKE, Liselotte, 1966: 'Zur Politik der deutschen Faschisten in Kolumbien 1933 bis 1941', in Helmuth Stoecker, ed., *Der deutsche Faschismus in Lateinamerika*. Berlin: Humboldt-Universität, pp. 125-144.

573   RODRÍGUEZ PLATA, Horacio, 1968: *La inmigración alemana al estado soberano de Santander en el siglo XIX: repercusiones socio-económicas de un proceso de transculturación*. Bogotá: Ediciones Tally, 273 pp.

See also: 986

Costa Rica

574   BOVING, Christine, 1986: *Deutsche Personennamen in Costa Rica. Eine namenkundliche Untersuchung als Dokument sprachlicher und sozio-kultureller Assimiliation und Integration deutscher Einwanderer in Mittelamerika*. Frankfurt and Bern: Lang, 688 pp.

575   FREIHERR VON HOUWALD, Götz, 1979: 'Die Deutschen in Costa Rica', in Hartmut Fröschle, ed., *Die Deutschen in Lateinamerika*. Tübingen and Basle: Horst Erdmann Verlag, pp. 577-596.

576   HERRERA BALHARRY, Eugenio, 1988: *Los alemanes y el estado cafetalero*. San José: Ed. Universidad Estatal a Distancia, 230 pp.

Cuba

577   BAĎURA, Bohumil, 1975: 'Sobre la inmigración alemana en Cuba durante la primera mitad del siglo XIX (1a parte)', *IAP*, yr. 9, pp. 71-105.

578   BAĎURA, Bohumil, 1976: 'Sobre la inmigración alemana en Cuba durante la primera mitad del siglo XIX (2a parte)', *IAP*, yr. 10, pp. 111-136

Dominican Republic

579   VEGA, Bernardo, 1985: *Nazismo, fascismo y falangismo en la República Dominicana*. Santo Domingo: Fundación Cultural Dominicana, 415 pp.

See also: 138; 139; 141; 1004; 1005; 1006; 1007

Ecuador

580   ANGERMEYER, Johanna, 1989: *My father's island: a Galapagos quest*. London: Viking, 302 pp.

581   TREHERNE, John, 1983: *The Galapagos affair*. London: Jonathan Cape, 223 pp.

582   ULLOA VERNIMEN, José, 1974: 'Los alemanes en el Ecuador', *VI*, 17/200, pp. 21-24.

583   WEILBAUER, Arthur, 1979: 'Die Deutschen in Ekuador', in Hartmut Fröschle, ed., *Die Deutschen in Lateinamerika*. Tübingen and Basle: Horst Erdmann Verlag, pp. 373-408.

584   WITTMER, Margaret, 1961: *Floreana*. London: Michael Joseph, 239 pp.

Guatemala

585   FRÖSCHLE, Hartmut and Ekkehard ZIPSER, 1979: 'Die Deutschen in Guatemala', in Hartmut Fröschle, ed., *Die Deutschen in Lateinamerika*. Tübingen and Basle: Horst Erdmann Verlag. pp. 597-606.

586   KING, Arden R., 1974: *Coban and the Verapaz. History and cultural process in northern Guatemala*. New Orleans: Tulane University (Middle America Research Institute Publication 37), 397 pp.

587   WAGNER, Regina, 1987: 'Actividades empresariales de los alemanes en Guatemala, 1870-1920', *MA*, 8/13, pp. 87-124.

See also: 1008; 1011; 1018

Mexico

588   BANKIER, David, 1988: 'Los exilados alemanes en México y sus vínculos con la comunidad judía (1942-1945)', in *Judaica latinoamericana: estudios histórico-sociales*. Jerusalem: Editorial Universitaria Magnes, Universidad

Hebrea, pp. 79-89

589   BERNECKER, Walther L., 1988: 'Los alemanes en el México decimonónico: cuantificación, estructura socioprofesional, posturas político-ideológicas', *JGSWGL*, vol. 25, pp. 385-414.

590   KÜHN, Joachim, 1965: 'Das Deutschtum in Mexiko um 1850', *JGSWGL*, vol. 2, pp. 335-372.

591   MENTZ DE BOEGE, Brígida M. von, 1988: 'Empresas y empresarios alemanes en México, 1821-1945', *JGSWGL*, vol. 25, pp. 1-31.

592   OESTE DE BOPP, Marianne, 1979: 'Die Deutschen in Mexico', in Hartmut Fröschle, ed., *Die Deutschen in Lateinamerika*. Tübingen and Basle: Horst Erdmann Verlag, pp. 475-564.

593   POHLE, Fritz, 1986: *Das mexikanische Exil: Ein Beitrag zur Geschichte der politisch-kulturellen Emigration aus Deutschland (1937-1946)*. Stuttgart: Metzler Verlag, 495 pp.

Nicaragua

594   HENDERSON, G.B., 1944: 'German colonial projects on the Mosquito coast, 1844-1848', *EHR*, vol. 59, pp. 257-71.

595   HOUWALD, Götz Freiherr von, 1975: *Los alemanes en Nicaragua*. Managua: Banco de América, 479 pp.

596   HOUWALD, Götz Freiherr von, 1979: 'Die Deutschen in Nikaragua', in Hartmut Fröschle, ed., *Die Deutschen in Lateinamerika*. Tübingen and Basle: Horst Erdmann Verlag, pp. 631-650.

597   HOUWALD, Götz Freiherr von, 1986: *Deutsches Leben in Nikaragua*. Bonn: Nikaragua-Gesellschaft, 422 pp.

Panama

598   PORCELL, Néstor G., 1974: 'La contribución de los científicos alemanes emigrados al desarrollo de las ciencias sociales en el Panamá del 30', *RL*, no. 221, pp. 43-52.

599   PORCELL, Néstor G., 1977: 'Imagen y influencia de los docentes alemanes en la naciente universidad y en la cultura nacional', *RL*, no. 261, pp. 1-29.

Paraguay

600   BUSSMANN, Claus, 1988: 'Die Krise der Deutschen Evangelischen Gemeinde zu Asunción nach dem Ersten Weltkrieg', *JGSWGL*, vol. 25, pp. 495-510.

601   BUSSMANN, Claus, 1989: *Treu deutsche evangelischen Gemeinde zu Asunción, Paraguay von 1893-1963*. Stuttgart: Franz Steiner, 182 pp.

602   FINKE, Theodor, 1989: *Leben und Arbeit deutschsprachiger Siedler in Südbrasilien und Paraguay*. Berlin and Bonn: West Kreuz-Verlag, 294 pp.

603   FORSTER, Bernhard, 1981: *Dr Bernhard Forster Kolonie Neu-Germania in Paraguay*. Commissions-Verlag der Aktiengesellschafft Pioner, 173 pp.

604   HOYER, Hans Jürgen, 1974: *Germans in Paraguay, 1881-1945: a study of cultural and social isolation*. PhD Thesis, American University.

605   ILG, Karl, 1989: *Das Deutschtum in Paraguay und Peru*. Vienna: Österreichische Landsmannschaft, 123 pp.

606   KRIER, Hubert, 1979: 'Die Deutschen in Paraguay', in Hartmut Fröschle, ed., *Die Deutschen in Lateinamerika*. Tübingen and Basle: Horst Erdmann Verlag, pp. 651-695.

607   SEIFERHELD, Alfredo M., 1986: *Nazismo y fascismo en el Paraguay. Los años de la guerra, 1939-1945*. Asunción: Editorial Histórica, 335 pp.

See also: 153; 154; 452

Peru

608   FRÖSCHLE, Hartmut and Georg PERTERSEN, 1979: 'Die Deutschen in Peru', in Hartmut Fröschle, ed., *Die Deutschen in Lateinamerika*. Tübingen and Basle: Horst Erdmann Verlag, pp. 696-741.

609   GERSTACKER, Friedrich, 1973: 'La colonia alemana en el Pozuzo', in *Viaje por el Perú*. Lima: Biblioteca Nacional, pp. 113-151.

610   WEIGL, Johann, 1963: 'Pozuzo, isla alemana en la selva peruana', *CP*, Jan-April, 328 pp.

See also: 192; 196; 197; 605; 1033

Puerto Rico

611   ACOSTA, Úrsula, 1985: 'Notas sobre la inmigración germánica a Puerto Rico a principios del siglo XIX', *RJ/SJu*, 1/1, pp. 139-145.

Uruguay

612   FRÖSCHLE, Hartmut and Hans Jürgen HOYER, 1979: 'Die Deutschen in Uruguay', in Hartmut Fröschle, ed., *Die Deutschen in Lateinamerika*. Tübingen and Basle: Horst Erdmann Verlag, pp. 742-766.

613   MEDINA PINTADO, María del Carmen, 1988: *La presencia alemana en el Uruguay, 1850-1930*. Montevideo: Ed. Gráficos, 282 pp.

614   MEEROFF BERHENS, Olaf, 1984: *La presencia alemana en Uruguay desde el descubrimiento de los territorios hasta la Primera Guerra Mundial*. Buenos Aires: Seminario de Estudios Latinoamericanos, 48 pp.

615   WINTER VON DAACK, T., 1979: *Los alemanes en el Uruguay*. Montevideo: Universidad de la República, Dirección General de Extensión Universitaria, 28 pp.

See also: 452; 879

Venezuela

616   BANKO, Catalina, 1988: 'Los comerciantes alemanes en La Guaira, 1821-1848', *JGSWGL*, vol. 25, pp. 61-81.

617   DUPOUY, Walter, 1968: 'Analogías entre la colonia Tovar, Venezuela y la colonia de Pozuzo en el Perú', *BACH*, no. 4, pp. 91-123.

618   FRÖSCHLE, Hartmut, 1979: 'Die Deutschen in Venezuela', in Hartmut Fröschle, ed., *Die Deutschen in Lateinamerika*. Tübingen and Basle: Horst Erdmann Verlag, pp. 767-805.

619   GILLIARD, Thomas, 1939: 'A "lost" German colony hidden away from the world in the Andean highlands of Venezuela', *NH* (June), pp.7-13.

620   HERWIG, Holger H., 1986: *Germany's vision of empire in Venezuela 1871-1914*. Princeton: Princeton University Press, 285 pp.

621   KOCH, Conrad, 1969: *La Colonia Tovar: Geschichte und Kultur einer alemannischen Siedlung in Venezuela*. Tübingen and Basle: Pharos-Verlag Hansrudolf Schwabe, 336 pp.

622 OLINTO CAMACHO, Óscar, 1984: 'Venezuela's national colonization program: the Tovar Colony, a German agricultural settlement', *JHG*, 10/3, pp. 279-89.

623 PERKINS, Renate Redlich, 1978: *Tovar German: linguistic study of a nineteenth century Alemannic dialect spoken in Venezuela.* PhD Thesis, University of Massachusetts.

624 SCHNEELOCH, Norbert H., 1979: 'Die Deutschen in Guayana', in Hartmut Fröschle, ed., *Die Deutschen in Lateinamerika.* Tübingen and Basle: Horst Erdmann Verlag, pp. 409-432.

625 SUÁREZ FIGUEROA, Naudy, 1976/7: 'Movimento socialista de obreros alemanes en el Venezuela de fines del siglo XIX', *BACH*, nos. 13/14, pp. 85-94.

626 WALTER, Rolf, 1982: 'Die Deutsche Kolonisation in Venezuela im 19. Jahrhundert. Einige Anmerkungen zu Tovar und Alexander Benitz', *LS*, vol. 9, pp. 29-47.

627 WALTER, Rolf, 1985: *Los alemanes en Venezuela desde Colón hasta Guzmán Blanco.* Caracas: Asociación Cultural Humbolt, 283 pp.

628 ZAWISZA, Leszek, 1980: *Colonia Tovar, tierra venezolana.* Caracas.

See also: 452

GREEK

Brazil

629   APOSTOLO, Paschoal, 1981: 'A colonização grega em Santa Catarina', *RIHGSC*, 3a fase, no. 3, pp. 83-89.

Mexico

630   PAPPATHEODOROU, Theodoro, 1987: *Memorias de un inmigrante griego llamado Pappatheodorou, Theodoro.* Jiquilpan, Michoacán: Centro de Estudios de la Revolución Mexicana "Lázaro Cárdenas" (Archivo de Historia Oral), 440 pp.

GYPSY

Argentina

631   GOBBI BELCREDI, Ana María, 1946: 'Los zíngaros', *RGA*, yr. 13, 20/150.

632   GARAY, Esteban, 1987: 'La presencia gitana en la Argentina', *TH*, 21/243, pp. 8-28.

HUNGARIAN

General

633   ÁCS, Tivadar, 1944: *Magyarok Latin Amerikában*. Budapest: Officina Képeskönyvek, 37 pp.

634   ANDERLE, Ádám, 1971: 'A felszabadulás és a latin-amerikai magyar emigráció', *TI*, April.

635   ANDERLE, Ádám, 1976: 'La emigración húngara a América Latina después de la derrota de la revolución de 1848-1849', *JGSWGL*, vol. 13, pp. 73-83.

636   ANDERLE, Ádám, 1979: 'Investigaciones acerca de la emigración húngara hacia América Latina', in *La emigración europea a la América Latina: fuentes y estado de investigación (informes presentados a la IV Reunión de Historiadores Latinoamericanistas Europeos)*. Berlin: Colloquium Verlag (Bibliotheca Ibero-Americana), pp. 229-240.

637   SZABÓ, László, 1982: *Magyar múlt Dél-Amerikában*. Budapest: Európa Könyviadó, 283 pp.

638   VARGA, Ilona, 1971: 'Latin-amerikai magyar telepek és külképviseleteink a gazdasági világválság idöszakában', *AUS*, No. 35, pp. 79-101

639   VARGA, Ilona, 1976: 'A kivándorlás irányváltozásai és a magyar kivándorlók beilleszkedése Latin-Amerikában a két világháború között', *AUS*, No. 35, 51 pp.

640   VARGA, Ilona, 1980: 'Los obreros húngaros emigrados en América Latina entre las dos guerras mundiales', *EL*, no. 7, pp. 67-82.

Argentina

641   CSIKÓS, Zsuzsa, 1988: 'Magyar szervezetek és újságok Argentínában (1945-1956)', *TI*, 42/7, pp. 78-82.

642   VARGA, Ilona, 1973: 'Adalékok az Argentínába kivándorló magyarok életének alakulásához a két világháború között', *AUS*, No. 46, pp. 45-59.

643   VARGA, Ilona, 1988: 'Magyar település Argentínában, a századelőn. A magyar kivándorlás helye a migrációs folyamatban', *TI*, 42/7, pp. 64-70.

Brazil

644   SCHMIDT, Judit, 1988: 'A São Pauló-i emigráció az 1950-es években', *TI*, 42/7, pp. 82-87.

Cuba

645   ANDERLE, Ádám, 1973: 'Az 1848-as magyar emigráció és Narciso López 1851-es kubai expediciója', *SK*, no. 3, pp. 687-710.

646   BUENO, Salvador, 1974: 'Los húngaros en Cuba', *RBNJM*, época 3, yr. 65, 16/2, pp. 195-215.

Dominican Republic

See: 139

Uruguay

647   KOVÁCS, Márta, 1988: 'Magyarok Uruguayban. Vázlat az 1930-as évekről', *TI*, 42/7, pp. 71-78.

ICELANDIC

Brazil

648   BJARNASON, Jóhann Magnús, 1905-8: *Brazilíufararnir* (2 vols.). Reykjavik, 240 pp.

649   JÓNSSON, Bergsteinn, 1975: 'Aðdragandi og upphaf vestuferða af íslandi á nítjándu öld', *AV*, no. 100, pp. 28-50.

650   KARTANSSON, Helgi Skúli, 1977: 'The onset of emigration from Iceland', *ASS*, 9/1-2, pp. 87-93.

651   ÞORSTEINSSON, Þorsteinn, 1937-8: *Æfintýrið. Frá Íslandi til Brasilíu. Fyrstu fólksflutningarnir frá Norðurlandi*. Reykjavik: Sigurgeir Friðriksson, 399 pp.

652   ÞORSTEINSSON, Þorsteinn, 1943: *Saga íslendinga í Vesturheimi*. Winnepeg: Þjoðræknisfélag. Íslendinga í Vesturheimi (Ch. 2, pp. 67-110).

ITALIAN

General

653   ANNINO, Antonio, 1976: 'El debate sobre la emigración y la expansión a la América Latina en los orígenes de la ideología imperialista en Italia (1861-1911)', *JGSWGL,* vol. 13, pp. 189-215.

654   CALAFUT, George, 1977: 'An analysis of Italian emigration statistics, 1876-1914', *JGSWGL,* vol. 14, pp. 310-332.

655   CANDIDO, Salvatore, 1976: 'La emigración política italiana a la América Latina (1820-1870)', *JGSWGL,* vol. 13, pp. 216-238.

656   CARMAGNANI, Marcello and Giovanna MANTELLI, 1979: 'Fuentes cuantitativas italianas relativas a la emigración italiana. Un análisis crítico', in *La emigración europea a la América Latina: fuentes y estado de investigación (informes presentados a la IV Reunión de Historiadores Latinoamericanistas Europeos).* Berlin: Colloquium Verlag (Bibliotheca Ibero-Americana), pp. 63-78.

657   DEAN, Warren, 1974: 'Remessas de dinheiro dos imigrantes italianos do Brasil, Argentina, Uruguay e Estados Unidos da América (1844-1914)', *ANH,* vol. 6, pp. 231-37.

658   FRANZINA, Emilio, 1979: *Merica! Merica! Emigrazione e colonizzazione nelle lettere dei contadini veneti in America Latina 1876-1902.* Milan: Feltrinelli Economica, 230 pp.

659   FRANZINA, Emilio, 1983: 'La terra, la violenza e la frontiera. Aspetti della immigrazione veneta in Brasile e Argentina attraverso le fonti italiane di fine Ottocento', in Emilio Franzina, ed., *Un altro Veneto: saggi e studi di storia dell'emigrazione nei secoli XIX e XX.* Padua: Francisci, pp. 549-598.

660   MOLINARI, Augusta, 1990: 'Fuentes para la historia de la emigración transoceánica italiana: la documentación sanitaria de a bordo', *EML,* no. 15-16, pp. 533-546.

661   RONCELLI, I.N., 1987: 'L'emigrazione italiana verso l'America Latina nel secondo dopoguerra (1945-1960)', *SRG,* 10/1, pp. 91-141.

662   SALVETTI, Patrizia, 1987: 'Il movimento migratorio italiano durante la prima guerra mondiale', *SE,* 24/87, pp. 282-294.

See also: 784

Argentina

663   ALLENDE, Andrés R., 1978: 'Primeros italianos en la colonización del desierto', *TC*, no. 23.

664   ARMUS, D., 1985: 'Mirando a los italianos. Algunas imágenes esbozadas por la élite en tiempos de la inmigración masiva', in Fernando Devoto and Gianfausto Rosoli, eds., *La inmigración italiana en la Argentina*. Buenos Aires: Editorial Biblos, pp. 95-104.

665   BAILY, Samuel L., 1978: 'The role of two newspapers in the assimilation of Italians in Buenos Aires and São Paulo, 1893-1913', *IMR*, 12/3, pp. 321-40.

666   BAILY, Samuel L., 1982: 'Las sociedades de ayuda mutua y el desarrollo de una comunidad italiana en Buenos Aires, 1858-1918', *DEC*, 21/84, pp. 485-514.

667   BAILY, Samuel L., 'Chain migration to Argentina: case studies of the Agnonesi and the Sirolesi', *SE*, 19/65, pp. 73-91.

668   BAILY, Samuel L., 1983: 'The adjustment of Italian immigrants in Buenos Aires and New York, 1870-1914', *AHR*, 88/2, pp. 281-305.

669   BAILY, Samuel L., 1985: 'Patrones de residencia de los italianos en Buenos Aires y Nueva York: 1880-1914', *EML*, no. 1, pp. 8-47.

670   BAILY, Samuel L., 1988: 'Cadenas migratorias de italianos a la Argentina: algunos comentarios', *EML*, no. 8, pp. 125-136.

671   BAILY, Samuel L. and Franco RAMELLA, 1988: *One family, two worlds: an Italian family's correspondence across the Atlantic, 1901-1922*. New Brunswick, New Jersey: Rutgers University Press, 251 pp.

672   BARBERO, María Inés and Susana FELDER, 1987: 'Industriales italianos y asociaciones empresariales en la Argentina. El caso de la Unión Industrial Argentina (1887-1930))', *EML*, no. 6-7, pp. 155-180.

673   BARBERO, María Inés, 1990: 'Grupos empresarios, intercambio, comercio e inversiones italianas en la Argentina. El caso de Pirelli (1910-1920)', *EML*, no. 15-16, pp. 311-342.

674   BARBERO, María Inés and Susana FELDER, 1988: 'El rol de los italianos en el nacimiento y desarrollo de las asociaciones empresarias en la

Argentina (1880-1930)', in Fernando J. Devoto and Gianfausto Rosoli, eds., *L'Italia nella società argentina*, Rome: Centro Studi Emigrazione, pp. 137-159.

675 BERNASCONI, Alicia, 1988: 'Inmigración italiana, colonización y mutualismo en el Centro-norte de la provincia de Santa Fe', in Fernando J. Devoto and Gianfausto Rosoli, eds., *L'Italia nella società argentina*. Rome: Centro Studi Emigrazione, pp. 178-189.

676 BERNASCONI, Alicia, 1990: 'Cofradías religiosas e identidad en la inmigración italiana en Argentina', *EML*, no. 14, pp. 211-224.

677 BIRINDELLI, Anna Maria, 1988: 'Stabilità e mutamenti della dinamica migratoria italiana all'estero negli ultimi decenni', in Fernando J. Devoto and Gianfausto Rosoli, eds., *L'Italia nella società argentina*. Rome: Centro Studi Emigrazione, pp. 102-123.

678 BLENGINO, V., 1980: 'Immigrazione italiana, letteratura e identità argentina', *NA*, 3, pp. 331-351

679 BOTELLI, José Juan, 1983: *Los italianos y descendientes en Salta*. Salta: Artes Gráficas, 221 pp.

680 CACOPARDO, María Cristina and José Luis MORENO, 1984: 'Características demográficas y ocupacionales de los migrantes italianos hacia Argentina (1880-1930)', *SE*, 21/75, pp. 277-193.

681 CACOPARDO, María Cristina, and José Luis MORENO, 1985: 'La emigración italiana a la Argentina entre 1880 y 1930. Las regiones de origen y el fenómeno del retorno', in *La inmigración a América Latina (primeras jornadas internacionales sobre la migración en América)*. México, DF: Instituto Panamericano de Geografía e Historia (Serie inmigración, tomo 2), pp. 43-50.

682 CACOPARDO, María Cristina, and José Luis MORENO, 1988: 'La migración italiana a Argentina: consideraciones metodológicas acerca de las fuentes estadísticas', *EML*, no. 10.

683 CALTAGIRONE, Luigi, 1985: 'La colonia italiana de Mendoza', *QASI*, no. 115.

684 CALTAGIRONE, L., 1985: *La colonia italiana di Mendoza*. Milan: Franco Angeli.

685 CANDELARESI, Ana Maria and Maria Teresa MONTERISI, 1989: *La presencia italiana en la ciudad de Córdoba, 1869-1895*, vol. 1. Córdoba, 152 pp.

686   CHIARAMONTE, José C., 1988: 'Notas sobre la presencia italiana en el litoral argentino en la primera mitad del siglo XIX', in Fernando J. Devoto and Gianfausto Rosoli, eds., *L'Italia nella società argentina*. Rome: Centro Studi Emigrazione, pp. 44-58.

687   CIBOTTI, Ema, 1988: 'Mutualismo y política en el estudio de caso. La Sociedad "Unione e Benevolenza" en Buenos Aires entre 1858 y 1865', in Fernando J. Devoto and Gianfausto Rosoli, eds., *L'Italia nella società argentina*. Rome: Centro Studi Emigrazione, pp. 241-265.

688   DE ROSA, Luigi, 1985: 'Emigrantes italianos, bancos y remesas. El caso argentino', in Fernando Devoto and Gianfausto Rosoli, eds., *La inmigración italiana en la Argentina*. Buenos Aires: Editorial Biblos, pp. 241-270.

689   DE ROSA, Luigi, 1988: 'L'emigrazione italiana in Argentina: un bilancio', in Fernando J. Devoto and Gianfausto Rosoli, eds., *L'Italia nella società argentina*. Rome: Centro Studi Emigrazione, pp. 73-89.

690   DEVOTO, Fernando J., 1984: 'Las sociedades italianas de ayuda mutua en Buenos Aires y Santa Fe. Ideas y problemas', *SE*, 21/75, pp. 320-342.

691   DEVOTO, Fernando J., 1985: 'Factores de expulsión y de atracción en la emigración italiana a la Argentina. El caso piamontés (1861-1914)', *CHR*, 1/2, pp. 10-33.

692   DEVOTO, Fernando J., 1988: 'Las cadenas migratorias italianas: algunas reflexiones a la luz del caso argentino', *EML*, no. 8, pp. 103-124.

693   DEVOTO, Fernando J., 1989: 'La primera élite política italiana de Buenos Aires', *SE*, 26/94, pp. 168-194.

694   DEVOTO, Fernando J., 1989: 'The origins of an Italian neighbourhood in Buenos Aires in the mid-nineteenth century', *JEUH*, 18/1, pp. 37-64.

695   DEVOTO, Fernando J., 1990: 'Catolicismo y anticlericalismo en un barrio italiano de Buenos Aires (La Boca) en la segunda mitad del siglo XIX', *EML*, no. 14, pp. 183-210

696   DEVOTO Fernando J. and Alejandro FERNÁNDEZ, 1988: 'Asociacionismo, liderazgo y participación en dos grupos étnicos en áreas urbanas de la Argentina finisecular. Un enfoque comparado', in Fernando J. Devoto and Gianfausto Rosoli, eds., *L'Italia nella società argentina*. Rome: Centro Studi Emigrazione, pp. 190-208.

697   FANESI, Pietro R., 1989: 'El anti-fascismo italiano en Argentina (1922-1945)', *EML*, no. 12, pp. 319-352.

698 FAVERO, Luigi, 1984: 'Le scuole delle società italiane di mutuo soccorso in Argentina (1866-1914)', SE, 21/75, pp. 343-380.

699 FAVERO, Luigi, 1989: 'Los scalabrinianos y los emigrantes italianos en Sudamérica', EML, no. 12, pp. 231-256.

700 FAVERO, Luigi and Luciano BAGGIO, 1985: 'Notas demográficas y sociológicas sobre la inmigración italiana en Argentina', in La inmigración a América Latina (primeras jornadas internacionales sobre la migración en América). México, DF: Instituto Panamericano de Geografía e Historia (Serie inmigración, tomo 2), pp. 75-84.

701 FONTANELLA DE WEINBERG, María Beatriz, 1984: 'Mantenimiento y cambio de lengua entre los italianos del sudoeste bonaerense', SE, 21/75, pp. 305-319.

702 FRID DE SILBERSTEIN, Carina, 1985: 'Mutualismo y educación en Rosario: las escuelas de Unione e Benevolenza y de la Sociedad Garibaldi (1874-1911)', EML, no. 1, pp. 77-97.

703 FRID DE SILBERSTEIN, Carina, 1987: 'Administración y política: los italianos en Rosario (1860-1890))', EML, no. 6-7, pp. 381-390.

704 FRID DE SILBERSTEIN, Carina Laura, 1988: 'Educación e identidad. Un análisis del caso italiano en la provincia de Santa Fe (1880-1920)', in Fernando J. Devoto and Gianfausto Rosoli, eds., L'Italia nella società argentina. Rome: Centro Studi Emigrazione, pp. 266-287.

705 GANDOLFO, Rómolo, 1988: 'Notas sobre la élite de una comunidad emigrada en cadena: el caso de los aragoneses', EML, no. 8, pp. 137-156.

706 GANDOLFO, Rómolo, 1988: 'Notas sobre la élite de una comunidad emigrada en cadena: el caso de los aragoneses', in Fernando J. Devoto and Gianfausto Rosoli, eds., L'Italia nella società argentina. Rome: Centro Studi Emigrazione, pp. 160-177.

707 GARCÍA, S., 1979-82: 'La inmigración italiana y española a través de las "historias de vida" de sus protagonistas', CINA, vol. 9, pp. 187-219.

708 GARIBALDI, Italo Américo, 1983: Los genoveses en Buenos Aires. La fé y el trabajo. Buenos Aires, 159 pp.

709 GENTILE, Emilio, 1985: 'Emigración e italianidad en Argentina, en los mitos de potencia del nacionalismo y del fascismo (1900-1930)', EML, no. 2, pp. 143-180.

710 HALPERÍN DONGHI, T., 1985: 'La inmigración italiana en la Argentina',

in Fernando Devoto and Gianfausto Rosoli, eds., *La inmigración italiana en la Argentina*. Buenos Aires: Editorial Biblos.

711   KLEIN, Herbert S., 1983: 'The integration of Italian immigrants into the United States and Argentina: a comparative analysis', *AHR*, 88/2, pp. 306-329.

712   LATTUCA, Ada and Alicia MORENO DE ANGELINO, 1989: *La inmigración italiana en el Litoral. El caso de Santa Fe*. México, DF : Instituto Panamericano de Geografía e Historia, 67 pp.

713   MERCADANTE, Luis, 1974: *La colectividad italiana en la Argentina*. Buenos Aires: Alzamor Editores, 293 pp.

714   MINICUCCI, M., 1989: *Qui e altrove: famiglie di Calabria e di Argentina*. Milan: Franco Angeli.

715   MORENO, José Luis and M.C. CACOPARDO, 1985: 'Características regionales, demográficas y ocupacionales de la inmigración italiana a la Argentina (1880-1930)', in Fernando Devoto and Gianfausto Rosoli, eds., *La inmigración italiana en la Argentina*. Buenos Aires: Editorial Biblos, pp. 63-85.

716   MORENO, José Luis, 1985: 'A propósito de los anarquistas italianos en la Argentina, 1880-1920', *CHR*, 2/4, pp. 42-63.

717   NASCIMBENE, Mario C.G., 1984: 'Analfabetismo e inmigración en la Argentina: el caso italiano', *SE*, 21/75, pp. 294-304.

718   NASCIMBENE, Mario, 1987: *Historia de los italianos en la Argentina, 1835-1920*. Buenos Aires: Centro de Estudios Migratorios Latino-americanos, 138 pp.

719   MELIS, Antonio, 1983: 'Figuras sociales de la inmigración italiana en el espejo de la narrativa argentina (1880-1930)', in *Capitales, empresarios y obreros europeos en América Latina (Actas del 6º Congreso de AHILA, Stockholm, 25-28 de Mayo 1981)*. Stockholm: Instituto de Estudios Latino-americanos (monografías, no. 8, tomo 2), pp. 780-794.

720   OLIVIERI, Mabel, 1987: 'Un siglo de legislación en materia de inmigración. Italia-Argentina (1860-1960)', *EML*, no. 6-7, pp. 225-248.

721   OSTUNI, M.R., 1985: 'Inmigración política italiana y movimiento obrero argentino', in Fernando Devoto and Gianfausto Rosoli, eds., *La inmigración italiana en la Argentina*. Buenos Aires: Editorial Biblos, pp. 105-126.

722   PAGANO, Nora, and Mario OPORTO, 1985: 'La conducta endogámica de

los grupos inmigrantes: pautas matrimoniales de los italianos en el barrio de La Boca en 1895', *EML*, no. 4, pp. 483-496.

723 PAGANO, Nora and Mario OPORTO, 1988: 'La conducta endogámica de los grupos inmigrantes: pautas matrimoniales de los italianos en el barrio de La Boca en 1895', in Fernando Devoto and Gianfausto Rosoli, eds., *L'Italia nella società argentina*. Rome: Centro Studi Emigrazione, pp. 90-101.

724 PÉREZ, Daniel, 1977: *Los italianos en Tandil*. Tandil, 176 pp.

725 PETRIELLA, Dionisio, 1976: *Diccionario biográfico italo-argentino*. Buenos Aires: Asociación Dante Alighieri, 771 pp,

726 PETRIELLA, Dionisio, 1979: *Augustín Rocca, en treinta años de recuerdos*. Buenos Aires: Asociación Dante Alighieri.

727 PETRIELLA, Dioniso, 1984: *Pioneros friulanos en la Argentina*. Buenos Aires: Asociación Dante Alighieri, 51 pp.

728 PRISLEI, Leticia, 1987: 'Inmigrantes y mutualismo. La sociedad italiana de Socorros Mutuos e instrucción de Belgrano (1879-1910)', *EML*, no.5, pp. 29-55.

729 REDONDO, Nélida, 1988: 'La Boca: evolución de un barrio étnico', *EML*, no. 9, pp. 269-294.

730 ROSOLI, Gianfausto, 1984: 'Le organizzazioni cattoliche italiane in Argentina (1866-1914)', *SE*, 21/75, pp. 381-408.

731 ROSOLI, Gianfausto, 1988: 'Il "conflitto sanitario" tra Italia e Argentina del 1911', in Fernando Devoto and Gianfausto Rosoli, eds., *L'Italia nella società argentina*. Rome: Centro Studi Emigrazione, pp. 288-310.

732 ROSSELLI, John, 1990: 'The opera business and the Italian immigrant community in Latin America, 1820-1930: the example of Buenos Aires', *PP*, no. 127, pp. 155-182.

733 RUGGIERO, Kristin, 1979: *Italians in Argentina: the Waldenses at Colonia San Gustavo, 1850-1910*. PhD Thesis, Indiana University.

734 RUGGIERO, Kristin, 1982: 'Gringo and creole, foreign and native values in a rural Argentine community', *JIASWA*, 24/2, pp. 163-82.

735 RUGGIERO, Kristin, 1986: 'Social and psychological factors in migration from Italy to Argentina: from the Waldensian valleys to San Gustavo', in Ira A. Glazier and Luigi De Rosa, eds., *Migration across time and nations:*

population mobility in historical contexts. New York and London: Holmes & Meier, pp. 160-173.

736   RUGGIERO, Kristin, 1988: *And here the world ends: the life of an Argentine village.* Stanford: Stanford University Press, 226 pp.

737   SARACENO, Elena, 1988: 'L'emigrazione fallita: rientri e carriere professionali dei friulani in Argentina', in Fernando Devoto and Gianfausto Rosoli, eds., *L'Italia nella società argentina.* Rome: Centro Studi Emigrazione, pp. 124-133.

738   SCARZANELLA, Eugenia, 1979: 'Immigrazione italiana e colonizzazione agricola in Argentina', in Renzo De Felice, ed., *Cenni storici sull'emigrazione italiana nelle Americhe e in Australia.* Milan: Franco Angeli Editore, pp. 15-36.

739   SCARZANELLA, Eugenia, 1981: 'L'industria argentina e gli immigrati italiani: nascita della borghesia bonarense', *AFLE,* vol. 15, pp. 356-412.

740   SCARZANELLA, Eugenia, 1983: 'La "febbre de grano": gli immigrati italiani e l'agricoltura argentina (1895-1914)', in Emilio Franzina, ed., *Un altro Veneto: saggi e studi di storia dell'emigrazione nei secoli XIX e XX.* Padua: Francisci, pp. 513-522.

741   SCARZANELLA, Eugenia, 1983: *Italiani d'Argentina: storie di contadini, industriali e missionari italiani in Argentina, 1850-1912.* Venice: Marsilio Editori, 175 pp.

742   SCARZANELLA, Eugenia, 1986: 'Trigo y plate (grano e soldi): L'emigrazione e l'agricoltura argentina (1870-1914)', *REMI,* 2/2, pp. 91-110.

743   SORI, E., 1985: 'Las causas económicas de la emigración italiana entre los siglos XIX y XX', in Fernando Devoto and Gianfausto Rosoli, eds., *La inmigración italiana en la Argentina.* Buenos Aires: Editorial Biblos, pp. 15-44.

744   VÁZQUEZ-PRESEDO, Vicente, 1971: 'The role of Italian migration in the development of the Argentine economy, 1875-1914', *EI,* 24/3-4, pp. 606-626.

745   VILLECCO, Adalberto F. and María Elena CURIA DE VILLECCO, 1988: 'Los acerneses en Tucumán. Un caso de cadena migratoria', *EML,* no. 8, pp. 83-102.

746   WEINBERG, Félix and Adriana S. EBERLE, 1988: 'Los abruzeses en Bahía Blanca. Estudio de cadenas migratorias', *EML,* no. 8, pp. 27-50.

747   ZAGO, Manrique, ed., 1983: *Argentina, la otra patria de los italianos.* Buenos Aires: Manrique Zago Ediciones, 220 pp.

748   ZAGO, Manrique, ed., 1987: *Los italianos en la Argentina en los últimos cincuenta años (1937-1987).* Buenos Aires: Manrique Zago Ediciones, 191 pp.

See also: 657; 665; 798; 1252

Brazil

749   ABREU, Adilson Avansi de, 1987: 'Italianos no Espírito Santo', in Luis A. De Boni, ed., *A presença italiana no Brasil.* Porto Alegre: Escola Superior de Teologia, pp. 187-202.

750   ALVIM, Zuleika M.F., 1983: 'Immigrazione e forza lavoro femminile in São Paulo (1880-1920)', in Emilio Franzina, ed., *Un altro Veneto: saggi e studi di storia dell'emigrazione nei secoli XIX e XX.* Padua: Francisci, pp. 491-512.

751   ALVIM, Zuleika M.F., 1986: *Brava gente! Os Italianos em São Paulo (1870-1920).* São Paulo: Brasiliense, 189 pp.

752   AZEVEDO, Thales de, 1979: 'The chapel as symbol: Italian colonization in southern Brazil', in M.L. Margolis and W.E. Carter, eds., *Brazil: anthropological perspectives.* New York: Columbia University Press, pp. 86-96.

753   AZEVEDO, Thales de, 1975: *Italianos e gauchos: os anos primeros da colonização italiana no Rio Grande do Sul.* Porto Alegre: Instituto Estadual do Livro (Série biênio de colonização e imigração), 310 pp.

754   AZZI, Riolando, 1987: *A igreja e os migrantes: a imigração e os primórdios de obra escalabriniana no Brasil (1884-1904), vol. I.* São Paulo: Edições Paulinas.

755   BALHANA, Altiva Pilatti, 1978: *Santa Felicidade: uma paróquia vêneta no Brasil.* Curitiba: Fundação Cultura, 155 pp.

756   BALHANA, Altiva Pilatti, 1987: 'Italianos no Paraná', in Luis A. De Boni, ed., *A presença italiana no Brasil.* Porto Alegre: Escola Superior de Teologia, pp. 120-144.

757   BANCK, Geert A., 1977: 'Estrategias de sobrevivencia en dos comunidades italianas en el Estado de Espírito Santo, Brasil', *BELC*, no. 23, pp. 21-39.

758   BASSANEZI, Maria Silvia C. Beozzo, 1987: 'Familia colona: italianos e seus descendentes numa fazenda de café paulista: 1895-1930', in Gianfausto Rosoli, ed., *Emigrazioni europee e popolo brasiliano*. Rome: Centro Studi Emigrazione, pp. 272-292.

759   BERETTA, Pier Luigi, 1975: 'Osservazioni sull'insediamento e sulle attività agricolo pastorali nella antica area coloniale italiana del Rio Grande do Sul, Brasil', *IAA*, 1/4, pp. 307-50.

760   BONATTI, Mário, 1974: *Aculturação linguistica numa colônia de imigrantes italianos de Santa Catarina, Brasil (1875-1974)*. São Paulo: Faculdade Salesiana de Filosofia, Ciências e Letras, 93 pp.

761   CENTRO STUDI EMIGRAZIONE, 1975: 'Note statistiche sui flussi migratori Italiani verso il Brasile', in G. Massa, ed., *Contributo alla storia della presenza italiana in Brasile*. Rome: Istituto Italo-Latino Americano, pp. 149-155.

762   CORSETTI, Berenice, 1987: 'O crime de ser italiana: a perseguição do Estado Novo', in Luis A. De Boni, ed., *A presença italiana no Brasil*. Porto Alegre: Escola Superior de Teologia, pp. 363-382.

763   COSTA, Rovílio, 1987: 'A literatura dialetal italiana como retrato de uma cultura', in Luis A. De Boni, ed., *A presença italiana no Brasil*. Porto Alegre: Escola Superior de Teologia, pp. 383-404.

764   DALL'ALBA, 1983: *Imigração italiana em Santa Catarina*. Caxias do Sul: Editora da Universidade de Caxias do Sul, 182 pp.

765   DE BONI, Luis, 1987: 'A colonização no Sul do Brasil através do relato de autoridades italianas', in Luis A. De Boni, ed., *A presença italiana no Brasil*. Porto Alegre: Escola Superior de Teologia, pp. 203-223.

766   DELHAES-GUENTHER, Dietrich von, 1975: 'La fondazione delle prime colonie italiane nel giudizio dei Tedeschi', in G. Massa, ed., *Contributo alla storia della presenza italiana in Brasile*. Rome: Istituto Italo-Latino Americano, pp. 43-54.

767   DERENZI, Luiz Serafim, 1974: *Os italianos no estado do Espírito Santo*. Rio de Janeiro: Editora Artenova, 177 pp.

768   DE ROSA, Luigi, 1987: 'L'emigrazione italiana in Brasile: un bilancio', in Gianfausto Rosoli, ed., *Emigrazioni europee e popolo brasiliano*. Rome: Centro Studi Emigrazione, pp. 153-167.

769   FROSI, Vitalina Maria and Ciro MIRORANZA, 1983: *Dialetos italianos: um perfil lingüístico dos ítalo-brasileiros do nordeste do Rio Grande do Sul.*

Caxias do Sul: Editora da Universidade de Caxias do Sul, 525 pp.

770   GIRON, Loraine Slomp, 1987: 'O cooperativismo vinícola gaúcho: a organização inicial', in Luis A. De Boni, ed., *A presença italiana no Brasil.* Porto Alegre: Escola Superior de Teologia, pp. 269-292.

771   GROSSELLI, Renzo M., 1986: *Vincere o morire: contadini trentini (veneti e lombardi) nelle foreste brasiliane. Parte 1: Santa Catarina, 1875-1900.* Trento: Edizione a Cura della Provincia Autonoma di Trento, 647 pp.

772   GROSSELLI, Renzo M., 1986: *Colonie imperiali nella terra del caffè. Contadini trentini (veneti e lombardi). Parte 2: Espirito Santo, 1874-1900.* Trento: Edizione a Cura della Provincia Autonoma di Trento, 471 pp.

773   GROSSELLI, Renzo M., 1988: *Dove cresce l'araucaria. Dal primero a Novo Tyrol. Contadini trentini (veneti e lombardi) nelle foreste brasiliane.* Trento, 337 pp.

774   HALL, Michael, 1979: 'Italianos em São Paulo (1880-1920)', *AMP*, vol. 29, pp. 201-215.

775   HALSEMA, Ineke van, 1991: *Housewives in the field: power, culture and gender in a south-Brazilian village.* Amsterdam: Centrum voor Studie en Documentatie van Latijns Amerika (CEDLA Latin American Studies, 59), 169 pp.

776   HUTTER, Lucy Maffei, 1986: *Imigração italiana em São Paulo en 1902-1914. O processo imigratório.* São Paulo: Instituto de Estudos Brasileiros/CESP, 248 pp.

777   ISENBURG, Teresa, 1987: '"Nois não tem direito de terras, tudo é para a gente da Oropa": l'immagine del Brasile nell'Italia di fine secolo', in Gianfausto Rosoli, ed., *Emigrazioni europee e popolo brasiliano.* Rome: Centro Studi Emigrazione, pp. 206-228.

778   MANFROI, Olivio, 1975: *A colonização italiana no Rio Grande do Sul: implicaçoes econômicas, políticas e culturais.* Porto Alegre: 218 pp.

779   MARTINELLI, Franco, 1988: *São Paulo: gli italiani. Integrazione sociale e diffusione culturale.* Rome: Bulzoni, 205 pp.

780   MARTINS, José de Souza, 1973: *A imigração e a crise do Brasil agrário.* São Paulo: Pioneira, 222 pp.

781   MARTINS, José de Souza, 1979: 'Mercato del lavoro ed emigrazione italiana in Brasile', in Renzo De Felice, ed., *Cenni storici sull'emigrazione italiana nelle Americhe e in Australia.* Milan: Franco Angeli Editore, pp.

165-184.

782   MARZANO, Luigi, 1985: *Colonos e missionários italianos nas florestas do Brasil.* Florianópolis: Editora de UFSC.

783   MERLER, Alberto, 1987: 'L'immigrazione sarda in Brasile e in America Latina', in Gianfausto Rosoli, ed., *Emigrazioni europee e popolo brasiliano.* Rome: Centro Studi Emigrazione, pp. 355-369.

784   MERLOTTI, Vânia, 1971: *O mito do padre entre descendentes italianos.* Porto Alegre: Escola Superior de Teologia, 103 pp.

785   PETRONE, Pasquale, 1987: 'A influência da imigração italiana nas origens da industrialização brasileira', in Luis A. De Boni, ed., *A presença italiana no Brasil.* Porto Alegre: Escola Superior de Teologia, pp. 489-507.

786   PELLIZZETTI, Beatriz, 1987: 'Colônia Cecília: anarquistas no Paraná', in Luis A. De Boni, ed., *A presença italiana no Brasil.* Porto Alegre: Escola Superior de Teologia, pp. 313-333.

787   PERCO, Daniela, 1983: 'Fonti orali ed emigrazione. Il caso del Rio Grande do Sul (Brasile)', in Emilio Franzina, ed., *Un altro Veneto: saggi e studi di storia dell' emigrazione nei secoli XIX e XX.* Padua: Francisci, pp. 360-386.

788   PEREIRA, João Baptista Borges, 1987: 'A migração italiana para o Brasil no pós-guerra: o núcleo colonial de Pedrinhas no Estado de São Paulo', in Gianfausto Rosoli, ed., *Emigrazioni europee e popolo brasiliano.* Rome: Centro Studi Emigrazione, pp. 370-376.

789   PIAZZA, Walter F., 1976: *A colonização italiana em Santa Catarina.* Florianópolis: Edição do Governo de Santa Catarina (Cultura catarinense série história), 88 pp.

790   POSENATO, Júlio, 1987: 'A arquitetura residencial rural norte-italiana e a imigração italiana no Rio Grande do Sul', in Luis A. De Boni, ed., *A presença italiana no Brasil.* Porto Alegre: Escola Superior de Teologia, pp. 452-488.

791   RODRÍGUEZ, Edgar, 1984: *Os anarquistas. Trabalhadores italianos no Brasil.* São Paulo: Global Editora, 187 pp.

792   RODRÍGUEZ, Edgar, 1985: *Lavoratori italiani in Brasile.* Salerno: Galzerano, 256 pp.

793   ROSOLI, Gianfausto, 1986: 'La crise des rélations entre l'Italie et le Brésil: la grande naturalization (1889-1896)', *REMI,* 2/2, pp. 69-90.

794   ROSOLI, Gianfausto, 1987: 'Le relazioni tra Italia e Brasile e le questioni dell'emigrazione (1889-1896)', in Gianfausto Rosoli, ed., *Emigrazioni europee e popolo brasiliano*. Rome: Centro Studi Emigrazione, pp. 180-205.

795   SANTOS, José Vicente Tavares dos, 1984: *Colonos do vinho: estudo sobre a subordinação do trabalho camponês ao capital*. São Paulo: Editora Hucitec, 182 pp.

796   SCARANO, Julita, 1987: 'A família e a mulher na imigração italiana em São Paulo', in Gianfausto Rosoli, ed., *Emigrazioni europee e popolo brasiliano*. Rome: Centro Studi Emigrazione, pp. 377-402.

797   TRENTO, Angelo, 1987: 'Emigrazione italiana e movimento operaio a São Paulo, 1890-1920', in Gianfausto Rosoli, ed., *Emigrazioni europee e popolo brasiliano*. Rome: Centro Studi Emigrazione, pp. 229-257.

798   TRENTO, Angelo, 1988: 'Argentina e Brasile come paesi di immigrazione nella pubblicistica italiana (1860-1920)', in Fernando Devoto and Gianfausto Rosoli, eds., *L'Italia nella società Argentina*, Rome: Centro Studi Emigrazione, pp. 211-240.

799   TRENTO, Angelo, 1989: 'L'emigrazione italiana in Brasile nel secondo dopoguerra (1946-1960)', *SE*, no. 95, pp. 388-415.

See also: 96; 657

Chile

800   CONTRERAS BATARCE, Juan and Gino VENTURELLI ABAD, 1988: *Un ensayo de colonización italiana en la Araucaria, 1903-1906*. Temuco: Edición Universidad de la Frontera, 138 pp.

801   DÍAZ, Carlos and Fredy CANCINO, 1988: *Italianos en Chile: breve historia de una inmigración*. Santiago: Ediciones Documentas, 140 pp.

802   ESTRADA, Baldomero, 1990: 'Notas sobre los genoveses en Valparaíso a través de los testamentos, 1850-1900', *EML*, no. 15-16, pp. 547-556.

803   MAINO PRADO, Valeria and G. Jean OEHNINGER GREENWOOD, 1987: 'La migración italiana en Chile: su distribución geográfica y su preferencia locacional en la ciudad de Santiago', *EML*, no. 6-7, pp. 199-224.

804   MAINO, Valeria, 1988: *Características de la inmigración italiana en Chile: 1880-1987*. Santiago: Edizioni Presenza, 72 pp.

805   ZALDÍVAR H., Paula, 1989: 'La Italia en sueños: imágenes, sentimientos e identidad de tres mujeres italianas inmigrantes en Chile', *EML*, no. 12, pp. 287-318.

See also: 128

Colombia

806   CARFAGNA, Umberto, 1985: *Italiani in Colombia*. Latina: AIES, 415 pp.

Costa Rica

807   AGUILAR BULGARELLI, Óscar, 1989: *La huelga de los tútiles, 1887-1889: un capítulo de nuestra historia social.* San José: Ed. Universidad Estatal a Distancia, 155 pp.

808   BARIATTI L., Rita, 1989: 'Inmigrantes italianos en Costa Rica: estudio de su integración mediante fuentes orales', *RH/SJ*, no. 20, pp. 105-131.

809   COLE, Darrye S., 1963: 'Italian colonists in Costa Rica', *AM*, 15/6, pp. 38-41.

810   FRANCESCHI, Temistocle, 1970: *Lingua e cultura di una comunità italiana in Costa Rica.* Florence: Valmartina, 369 pp.

811   WEIZMANN, H.G., 1984: *Rural development of reclaimed land by migrants. A case study of land settlement in Costa Rica: San Vito de Java.* Geneva: Intergovernmental Committee for Migration, 48 pp.

See also: 133

Ecuador

812   ULLOA VERNIMEN, José, 1974: 'Los italianos en el Ecuador', *VI*, 17/202, pp. 30-36.

Mexico

813   BOHME, F.G., 1959: 'The Italians in Mexico: a minority's contribution', *PHR*, vol. 28, pp. 1-18.

814   SARTOR, Mario and Flavia URSINI, 1983: *Cent' anni d'emigrazione. Una còmunità veneta sugli altipiani del Messico.* Crocetta del Montello

(Treviso), 327 pp.

815   ZILLI, José B., 1981: *Italianos en México. Documentos para la historia de los colonos italianos en México.* México, DF: Ediciones San José, 515 pp.

816   ZILLI, José B., 1986: *Braceros italianos para México. (La historia olvidada de la huelga de 1900).* Xalapa: Ed. Universidad Veracruzana, 93 pp.

Paraguay

817   MAJAVACCA, José and Juan Francisco PÉREZ ACOSTA, 1951: *El aporte italiano al progreso del Paraguay (1527-1930).* Asunción: Biblioteca de la Sociedad Científica del Paraguay, 219 pp.

Peru

818   ALFARO VALLEJOS, Julia, 1989: *Los pescadores italianos de Chucuito.* Lima: Banco de Desarrollo (BANDESCO), 84 pp.

819   BELLONE, Bruno, 1984: 'La inmigración agrícola italiana en el Perú', in Bruno Bellone, ed., *Presencia italiana en el Perú.* Lima: Istituto Italiano di Cultura, pp. 103-203.

820   CHIARAMONTE, Gabriella, 1983: 'La migración italiana en América Latina. El caso peruano', *AP*, no. 13, pp. 15-36.

821   CHIARAMONTE, Gabriella, 1983: 'Empresarios italianos y proceso de industrialización en el Perú entre finales del siglo XIX y la primera guerra mundial', in *Capitales, empresarios y obreros europeos en América Latina (Actas del 6º Congreso de AHILA, Stockholm, 25-28 de Mayo 1981).* Stockholm: Instituto de Estudios Latinoamericanos (monografías, no. 8, tomo 2), pp. 551-599.

822   CICCARELLI, Orazio A., 1988: 'Fascist propaganda and the Italian community in Peru during the Benavides Regime, 1933-39', *JLAS*, 20/2, pp. 361-388.

823   CORBELLA, Paola María, 1984: 'La inmigración italiana en el Perú durante la época del guano', in Bruno Bellone, ed., *Presencia italiana en el Perú.* Lima: Istituto Italiano di Cultura, pp. 233-241.

824   PARIS, Robert, 1982: 'Los italianos en el Perú', *AP*, 7/12, pp. 33-45.

825   WORRALL, Janet E., 1972: *Italian immigration to Peru, 1860-1914*. PhD Thesis, Indiana University.

826   WORRALL, Janet E., 1976: 'Growth and assimilation of the Italian colony in Peru, 1860-1914', *SE*, 13/41, pp. 41-61.

Puerto Rico

827   HERNÁNDEZ, Pedro Juan, 1976: 'Los inmigrantes italianos de Puerto Rico durante el siglo XIX', *AIH*, 3/2.

Uruguay

828   CANDIDO, Salvatore, n.d: *Presenza d'Italia in Uruguay nel secolo XIX. Contributo alla storia delle relazioni fra gli Stati italiani e l'Uruguay dal 1835 al 1860*. Montevideo: Istituto Italiano di Cultura, 130 pp.

829   CESIO, Enrique A., 1986: 'Los Italianos de Salto en 1906', *HH*, 6/16, pp. 67-73.

830   CORREDERA ROSSI, Ketty, 1989: *Inmigración italiana en el Uruguay, 1860-1920*. Montevideo: Proyección, 139 pp.

831   DÍAS KAYEL, Bárbara, 1985/6: 'Los orígenes de la colonización valdense', *HH*, 3/13, pp. 21-29.

832   FILGUEIRA, Carlos and Juan RIAL, 1983: *Gli immigrati italiani nella construzioal del "Welfare State" in Uruguay all'inizio del secolo*. Milan: Franco Angeli, 52 pp.

833   MAROCCO, Gianni, 1986: *Sull'altra sponda del Plata. Gli italiani in Uruguay*. Milan: Franco Angeli, 206 pp.

834   RODRÍGUEZ VILLAMIL, Silvia and Graciela SAPRIZA, 1982: *La inmigración europea en el Uruguay: los italianos*. Montevideo: Ediciones de la Banda Oriental, 155 pp.

See also: 657

Venezuela

835   MASTRELLI, Roberto, 1984: *La segunda generación en Venezuela. Una encuesta entre los hijos de los italianos*. Caracas: Centro de Estudios de Pastoral y Asistencia Migratoria, 199 pp.

836 SANTANDER LEYA, Gustavo and Rafael SANTANDER GARRIDO, 1978: *Los italianos: formadores de la nacionalidad y del desarrollo económico de Venezuela.* Valencia, Venezuela: Vadell Editores, 284 pp.

837 VANNINI DE GERULEWICZ, Marisa, 1980: *Italia y los italianos en la historia y en la cultura de Venezuela.* Caracas: Ediciones de la Biblioteca, 633 pp.

838 VANNINI DE GERULEWICZ, Marisa, 1983: 'Panorama histórico de la presencia de los italianos en Venezuela desde el siglo XIX', in *Migraciones latinas y formación de la nación latinoamericana.* Caracas: Universidad Simón Bolívar, pp. 297-310.

JEWISH

Bibliographies

839   BASSECHES, Bruno, 1961: *Bibliografia das fontes de história dos judeus no Brasil, incluindo obras sobre judaísmo publicadas no Brasil.* Rio de Janeiro, mimeo, 70 pp.

840   BILSKY, Edgardo, and Gabriel TRAJTENBERG, 1987: *Bibliografia temática sobre judaísmo argentino: el movimiento obrero judío en la Argentina.* Buenos Aires: Centro de Documentación e Información sobre Judaísmo Argentino "Marc Turkow"; vol. 1: 293 pp., vol. 2: 344 pp.

841   ELKIN, Judith Laikin and Ana Lya SATER, 1991: *Latin American Jewish studies: an annotated guide to literature.* New York: Greenwood Press, 272 pp.

842   KLEINER, Alberto, ed., 1985: *Bibliografía argentina sobre temática judía.* Buenos Aires: Instituto Hebreo de Ciencias.

843   MARGULIES, Marcos, 1974: *Judaica brasiliensis: repertório bibliográfico comentado dos livros relacionados com o judaísmo e questões afins, publicados no Brasil desde os primórdios até o presente.* Rio de Janeiro: Editora Documentário, 159 pp.

844   SABLE, Martin H., 1978: *Latin American Jewry: a research guide.* Cincinnati: Hebrew Union College Press, 633 pp.

845   SCHLESINGER, Hugo, 1989: *Judaica brasiliensis III, 1984-1988: repertório bibliográfico das publicações relacionadas com o judaísmo e questões afins.* São Paulo: Federação Israelita do Estado de São Paulo, 165 pp.

846   SCHRADER, Achim and Thomas BLANK, 1989: 'Bibliographie zum Studium des deutschen Judentums in Lateinamerika', in Achim Schrader and Karl Heinrich Rengstorf, eds. *Europäische Juden in Lateinamerika.* St. Ingbert: Werner J. Röhrig Verlag, pp. 473-503.

General

847   AVNI, Haim, 1987: 'Latin America and the Jewish refugees: two encounters, 1935 and 1938', in Judith Laikin Elkin and Gilbert W Merkx, eds., *The Jewish presence in Latin America.* Boston: Allen and Unwin, pp.

45-70.

848   BANKIER, David, 1989: 'Die Beziehungen zwischen deutschen jüdischen Flüchtlingen und deutschen politischen Exilierten in Südamerika', in Achim Schrader and Karl Heinrich Rengstorf, eds., *Europäische Juden in Lateinamerika*. St. Ingbert: Werner J. Röhrig Verlag, pp. 213-225.

849   BELLER, Jacob, 1969: *Jews in Latin America*. New York: Jonathan David, 303 pp.

850   BRISTOW, Edward J., 1982: *Prostitution and prejudice: the Jewish fight against white slavery, 1870-1939*. Oxford: Clarendon Press, 340 pp.

851   DELLA PERGOLA, Sergio, 1987: 'Demographic trends of Latin American Jewry', in Judith Laikin Elkin and Gilbert W Merkx, eds., *The Jewish presence in Latin America*. Boston: Allen and Unwin, pp. 85-134.

852   ECK, Nathan, 1957: 'The rescue of Jews with the aid of passports and citizenship papers of Latin American states', *YVS*, vol. 1, pp. 136-141.

853   ELKIN, Judith Laikin, 1980: *Jews of the Latin American republics*. Chapel Hill: University of North Carolina Press, 298 pp.

854   ELKIN, Judith Laikin, 1980: *Latin American Jewish studies*. Cincinnati: American Jewish Archives, 53 pp.

855   ELKIN, Judith Laikin, 1982: 'A demographic profile of Latin American Jewry', *AJA*, 34/2, pp. 231-248.

856   ELKIN, Judith Laikin, 1983: 'The reception of the muses in the circum-Caribbean', in Jarrell C. Jackman and Carla M. Borden, eds., *The muses flee Hitler: cultural transfer and adoption, 1930-1945*. Washington, D.C.: Smithsonian Institute Press, pp. 291-302.

857   ELKIN, Judith Laikin, 1984: 'Latin American Jewry today', in *American Jewish Year Book: 1985*. New York and Philadelphia, pp. 3-49.

858   ELKIN, Judith Laikin, 1987: 'The evolution of the Latin American-Jewish communities: retrospect and prospect', in Judith Laikin Elkin and Gilbert W. Merkx, eds., *The Jewish presence in Latin America*. Boston: Allen and Unwin, pp. 309-323.

859   GLICKMAN, Nora, 1982: 'The Jewish white slave trade in Latin American writing', *AJA*, 34/2, pp. 178-189.

860   HOROWITZ, Irving Louis, 1976: 'Jewish ethnicity and Latin American nationalism', in Abdul A. Said and Luis R. Simmons, eds., *Ethnicity in an*

international context: the politics of disassociation. New Brunswick, NJ: Transaction Books, pp. 92-109.

861   LEVINE, Robert M., 1987: 'Adaptive strategies of Jews in Latin America', in Judith Laikin Elkin and Gilbert W. Merkx, eds., *The Jewish presence in Latin America.* Boston: Allen and Unwin, pp. 71-84.

862   LEVY, Daniel C., 1987: 'Jewish education in Latin America', in Judith Laikin Elkin and Gilbert W. Merkx, eds., *The Jewish presence in Latin America.* Boston: Allen and Unwin, pp. 157-186.

863   MÜHLEN, Patrick von zur, 1989: 'Politisches Engagement und jüdische Identität im lateinamerikaniscen Exil', in Achim Schrader and Karl Heinrich Rengstorf, eds., *Europäische Juden in Lateinamerika.* St. Ingbert: Werner J. Röhrig Verlag, pp. 242-249.

864   NES EL, Moshe, 1987: *Estudios sobre el judaísmo latinoamericano.* Buenos Aires: Ediciones Ultra, 152 pp.

865   POHLE, Fritz, 1989: '"Freies Deutschland" und Zionismus. Exil-kommunistische Bündnisbemühungen um die jüdische Emigration', in Achim Schrader and Karl Heinrich Rengstorf, eds., *Europäische Juden in Lateinamerika.* St. Ingbert: Werner J. Röhrig Verlag, pp. 226-241.

866   RENGSTORF, Karl Heinrich, 1989: 'Deutschsprachige Literatur deutsch-jüdischer Emigranten in Lateinamerika und was sich in ihr reflektiert', in Achim Schrader and Karl Heinrich Rengstorf, eds., *Europäische Juden in Lateinamerika.* St. Ingbert: Werner J. Röhrig Verlag, pp. 182-197.

867   SCHERS, David, 1987: 'Culture, identity and community', in Judith Laikin Elkin and Gilbert W. Merkx, eds., *The Jewish presence in Latin America.* Boston: Allen and Unwin, pp. 285-296.

868   SCHRADER, Achim, 1989: '¿Desaparecidos sin dejar huella? La República Federal de Alemania y los migrantes judío-alemanes en la América Latina', *EML*, no. 11, pp. 5-18.

869   SCHRADER, Achim, 1989: 'Spurlos verschwunden? Deutsche Juden in Lateinamerika', in Achim Schrader and Karl Heinrich Rengstorf, eds., *Europäische Juden in Lateinamerika.* St. Ingbert: Werner J. Röhrig Verlag, pp. 15-34.

870   SCHMELZ, U.O. and Sergio DELLA PERGOLA, 1985: 'The demography of Latin American Jewry', *AJYB*, vol. 85, pp. 51-102.

871   SOSNOWSKI, Saúl, 1986: 'Literatura judeo-latinoamericana: sobre fronteras étnicas y nacionales', in *Ninth World Congress of Jewish Studies,*

(Jerusalem, Aug. 4-12, 1985), Div. B, vol. 3. Jerusalem: World Congress of Jewish Studies, pp. 279-284.

872   SOSNOWSKI, Saúl, 1987: 'Latin American-Jewish writers: protecting the hyphen', in Judith Laikin Elkin and Gilbert W. Merkx, eds., *The Jewish presence in Latin America.* Boston: Allen and Unwin, p. 297-308.

873   STRAUSS, Herbert A., 1989: 'Jüdische Emigration als Epochenproblem', in Achim Schrader and Karl Heinrich Rengstorf, eds., *Europäische Juden in Lateinamerika.* St. Ingbert: Werner J. Röhrig Verlag, pp. 35-46.

874   SYRQUIN, Moisés, 1985: 'The economic structure of Jews in Argentina and other Latin American countries', *JSS*, vol. 47, no. 2, pp. 115-134.

See also: 187; 455; 457; 458; 463; 935

Argentina

875   ANSEL, Bernard D., 1969: *The beginning of the modern Jewish community in Argentina.* PhD Thesis, University of Kansas.

876   ARCUSCHIN, Maria, 1986: *De Ucrania a Basavilbaso.* Buenos Aires: Marymar Ediciones, 96 pp.

877   AVNI, Haim, 1983: *Argentina y la historia de la inmigración judía (1810-1950).* Buenos Aires: Editorial Universitaria Magnes and Jerusalem: Universidad Hebrea de Jerusalén, 593 pp.

878   AVNI, Haim, 1983: 'La agricultura judía en la Argentina: ¿éxito o fracaso?', *DEC*, 22/88.

879   BANKIER, David, 1989: 'Los exiliados alemanes y los refugiados judíos centroeuropeos en Argentina y Uruguay', *EML*, no. 11, pp. 49-60.

880   BANKIER, David, 1989: 'Deutsch-jüdische Symbiose bis 1933, argentinisch-jüdische Symbiose bis 1950', in Achim Schrader and Karl Heinrich Rengstorf, eds., *Europäische Juden in Lateinamerika.* St. Ingbert: Werner J. Röhrig Verlag, pp. 250-264.

881   BILSKY, Edgardo, 1989: 'Etnicidad y clase obrera: la presencia judía en el movimiento obrero argentino', *EML*, no. 11, pp. 27-48.

882   CORBIÈRE, Emilio J., 1987: 'Perón y los judíos', *TH*, 22/252, pp. 6-35.

883   DUJOVNE, Miriam S, Ana BERCZ, Abraham MILLER and Jaime BARYLKO, 1986: *Los judíos en la Argentina.* Buenos Aires: Betenu.

884   ELAZAR, Daniel J. and Peter MEDDING, 1983: *Jewish communities in frontier societies: Argentina, Australia, and South Africa.* New York: Holmes and Meir, pp. 61-134.

885   ELKIN, Judith Laikin, 1978: 'Goodnight, sweet gaucho: a revisionist view of the Jewish agricultural experiment in Argentina', *AJHQ*, 67, pp. 208-23.

886   ELKIN, Judith Laikin, 1986: 'The Jewish community of Buenos Aires: dilemmas of democratization', in *Ninth World Congress of Jewish Studies (Jerusalem, Aug. 4-12, 1985), Div. B, vol. 3.* Jerusalem: World Congress of Jewish Studies, pp. 345-352.

887   ELKIN, Judith Laikin, 1987: 'Anti-semitism in Argentina', in Jehuda Reinharz, ed., *Living with anti-semitism: modern Jewish responses.* Hanover, NH and London: University Press of New England, pp. 333-348.

888   ELKIN, Judith Laikin, 1989: 'Mit Antisemitismus leben. Das argentinische Ambiente', in Achim Schrader and Karl Heinrich Rengstorf, eds., *Europäische Juden in Lateinamerika.* St. Ingbert: Werner J. Röhrig Verlag, pp. 393-411.

889   EVEN-SHOSHAN, Israel, 1987: 'Informal Jewish education in Argentina', in Judith Laikin Elkin and Gilbert W. Merkx, eds., *The Jewish presence in Latin America.* Boston: Allen and Unwin, pp. 271-284.

890   GARDIOL, Rita, 1986: 'The move to the city as seen in the works of Tiempo, Eichelbaum and Verbitsky', in *Ninth World Congress of Jewish Studies (Jerusalem, Aug. 4-12, 1985), Div. B, vol. 3.* Jerusalem: World Congress of Jewish Studies, pp. 293-300.

891   GELDSTEIN, Rosa N., 1988: 'Matrimonios mixtos en la población judía de Salta. Un análisis socio-demográfico', *EML*, no. 9, pp. 217-238.

892   HARAP, Louis, 1984: 'Jews in Argentine drama, 1900-1918', *AJA*, vol. 36, pp. 136-150.

893   HORL GROENEWOLD, Sabine, 1989: 'Europäische Juden in Argentinien. Bild und Selbstbild', in Achim Schrader and Karl Heinrich Rengstorf, eds., *Europäische Juden in Lateinamerika.* St. Ingbert: Werner J. Röhrig Verlag, pp. 198-212.

894   HORL GROENEWOLD, Sabine, 1989: 'Judíos europeos en la Argentina: imagen y autoimagen', *EML*, no. 11, pp. 85-96.

895   HOROWITZ, Irving Louis, 1962: 'The Jewish community in Buenos Aires', *JSS*, 24/4, pp. 195-222.

896   ITZIGSOHN, Sara, et al., 1985: *Integración y marginalidad: historia de vidas de inmigrantes judíos en la Argentina.* Buenos Aires: Pardés.

897   JACKISCHE, Carlota, 1989: 'Die Einwanderungspolitik Argentiniens gegenüber den Juden 1933-1945', in Achim Schrader and Karl Heinrich Rengstorf, eds., *Europäische Juden in Lateinamerika.* St. Ingbert: Werner J. Röhrig Verlag, pp. 69-76.

898   KAUFMAN, Edy and Beatriz CYMBERKNOPF, 1989: 'La dimensión judía en la represión durante el gobierno militar en la Argentina (1976-1983)', in Leonardo Senkman, ed., *El antisemitismo en la Argentina.* Buenos Aires: Centro Editor de América Latina, pp. 235-273.

899   KLEINER, Alberto, ed., 1984: *El partido peronista y el antisemitismo.* Buenos Aires: Libreros y Editores del Polígono, 78 pp.

900   KOWALSKA, Marta, 1988: 'Los judíos y el movimiento migratorio de Polonia a la Argentina en los años 1918-1939', in *Judaica latinoamericana; estudios histórico-sociales.* Jerusalem: Editorial Universitaria Magnes, Universidad Hebrea, pp. 41-56.

901   KOWALSKA, Marta, 1989: 'La emigración judía de Polonia a la Argentina en los años 1918-1939', *EL*, no. 12, pp. 249-272.

902   LERNER, Natán, 1989: 'Las raíces ideológicas del antisemitismo en la Argentina y el nacionalismo', in Leonardo Senkman, ed., *El antisemitismo en la Argentina.* Buenos Aires: Centro Editor de América Latina, pp. 195-207.

903   LEWIN, Boleslao, 1971: *Cómo fue la inmigración judía a la Argentina.* Buenos Aires: Editorial Plus Ultra, 207 pp.

904   LEWIN, Boleslao, 1974: *La colectividad judía en la Argentina.* Buenos Aires: Alzamor Editores, 232 pp.

905   LIBERMAN, José, 1959: *Tierra soñada: episodios de la colonización agraria judía en la Argentina (1889-1959).* Buenos Aires: Laserre.

906   LIEBMAN, Seymour B., 1981: 'Argentine Jews and their institutions', *JSS*, vol. 43, pp. 311-328.

907   LINDSTROM, Naomi, 1989: *Jewish issues in Argentine literature: from Gerchunoff to Szichman.* Columbia: University of Missouri Press, 205 pp.

908   McGEE DEUTSCH, Sandra, 1986: 'The Argentine right and the Jews, 1919-1933', *JLAS*, 18/1, pp. 113-34.

909   MERKX, Josep and Jack Twiss QUARLES, 1989: '"Ich hab noch einen Koffer in Berlin". Deutsch-jüdische Einwanderer der ersten Generation in Argentinien', in Achim Schrader and Karl Heinrich Rengstorf, eds., *Europäische Juden in Lateinamerika*. St. Ingbert: Werner J. Röhrig Verlag, pp. 157-181.

910   MIRELMAN, Victor A., 1971: 'A note on Jewish settlement in Argentina, 1881-1892', *JSS*, vol. 33, pp. 3-12.

911   MIRELMAN, Victor A., 1978: 'Jewish life in Buenos Aires before the east European immigration (1860-1890)', *AJHQ*, 67/3, pp. 195-207.

912   MIRELMAN, Victor A., 1982: 'Early Zionist activities among Sephardim in Argentina', *AJA*, 34/2, pp. 190-205.

913   MIRELMAN, Victor A., 1987: 'Sephardic immigration to Argentina prior to the Nazi period', in Judith Laikin Elkin and Gilbert W. Merkx, eds., *The Jewish presence in Latin America*. Boston: Allen and Unwin, pp. 13-32.

914   MIRELMAN, Victor A., 1988: *En búsqueda de una identidad: los inmigrantes judíos en Buenos Aires, 1890-1930*. Buenos Aires: Milá, 426 pp.

915   MIRELMAN, Victor A., 1990: *Jewish Buenos Aires: in search of identity*. Detroit: Wayne State University Press, 301 pp.

916   NORMAN, Theodore, 1985: *An outstretched arm: a history of the Jewish Colonization Society*. London: Routledge & Kegan Paul, 326 pp.

917   RIVANERA CARLES, Federico, 1986: *Las escuelas judías comunistas en Argentina: documentación secuestrada por la policía*. Buenos Aires: Biblioteca de Formación Política, 64 pp.

918   ROSENSWAILKE, Ira, 1960: 'The Jewish population in Argentina: census and estimate, 1887-1947', *JSS*, 22/4, pp. 195-214.

919   SADOW, Stephen A., 1982: 'Judíos y gauchos: the search for identity in Argentine-Jewish literature', *AJA*, 34/2, pp. 164-177.

920   SCHECHNER, Tzvi, 1986: 'La creación de organizaciones comunitarias sobre la base de "asociaciones de entierro" en el judaísmo ashkenazi de Buenos Aires y México, DF', in *Ninth World Congress of Jewish Studies (Jerusalem, Aug. 4-12, 1985), Div. B, vol. 3*. Jerusalem: World Congress of Jewish Studies, pp. 241-248.

921   SCHENKOLOESKI, Silvia, 1988: 'Cambios en la relación de la Organización Sionista Mundial hacia la comunidad judía y el movimiento sionista en

la Argentina, hasta 1948', in *Judaica latinoamericana; estudios histórico-sociales*. Jerusalem: Editorial Universitaria Magnes, Universidad Hebrea, pp. 149-166.

922   SCHWARTZ, Kessel, 1978: 'Anti-semitism in modern Argentine fiction', *JSS*, vol. 40, pp. 131-140.

923   SEGAL, Bernard, 1987: 'Jews and the Argentine center: a middleman minority', in Judith Laikin Elkin and Gilbert W. Merkx, eds., *The Jewish presence in Latin America*. Boston: Allen and Unwin, pp. 201-218.

924   SENKMAN, Leonardo, 1983: *La identidad judía en la literatura argentina*. Buenos Aires: Pardes, 493 pp.

925   SENKMAN, Leonardo, 1986: 'La política migratoria de Argentina y los refugiados judíos, ucranianos y croatas (1945-1948)', in *Ninth World Congress of Jewish Studies (Jerusalem, Aug. 4-12, 1985), Div. B, vol. 3*. Jerusalem: World Congress of Jewish Studies, pp. 225-232.

926   SENKMAN, Leonardo, 1987: 'Argentine culture and Jewish identity', in Judith Laikin Elkin and Gilbert W. Merkx, eds., *The Jewish presence in Latin America*. Boston: Allen and Unwin, pp. 255-270.

927   SENKMAN, Leonardo, 1989: 'Argentinien und der Holocaust. Die Einwanderungspolitik und die Frage der Flüchtlinge 1933-1945', in Achim Schrader and Karl Heinrich Rengstorf, eds., *Europäische Juden in Lateinamerika*. St. Ingbert: Werner J. Röhrig Verlag, pp. 49-68.

928   SENKMAN, Leonardo, ed., 1989: *El antisemitismo en la Argentina*. Buenos Aires: Centro Editor de América Latina, 476 pp.

929   SENKMAN, Leonardo, 1989: 'El antisemitismo bajo dos experiencias democráticas: Argentina 1959-1966 y 1973-1976', in Leonardo Senkman, ed., *El antisemitismo en la Argentina*. Buenos Aires: Centro Editor de América Latina, pp. 11-193.

930   SENKMAN, Leonardo and Eliahu DANIEL, 1984: *La condición judeo-argentina en los años sesenta*. Buenos Aires: Ediciones J.N. Bialik.

931   SIMONOVICH, Javier, 1989: 'Desaparecidos y antisemitismo en la Argentina, 1976-1983. Las respuestas de la comunidad judía', in Leonardo Senkman, ed., *El antisemitismo en la Argentina*. Buenos Aires: Centro Editor de América Latina, pp. 310-328.

932   SISKAL, Dov, 1989: '"Die Presse": the oldest Jewish daily in the world', *QE*, no. 5, pp. 70-77.

933   SOFER, Eugene F., 1982: *From Pale to Pampa: a social history of the Jews of Buenos Aires*. New York: Holmes & Meier, 165 pp.

934   SPITTER, Arnold, 1989: 'Corrientes antisemitas y política de inmigración en la Argentina de los años treinta y cuarenta', *EML*, no. 11, pp. 19-26.

935   SYRQUIN, Moshe, 1985: 'The economic structure of Jews in Argentina and other Latin American countries', *JSS*, vol. 47, no. 2, pp. 115-134.

936   TRENTALANCE DE KIPREOS, Silvia, 1988: 'El sentido de la "Argentinidad" en Alberto Gerchunoff', in *Judaica latinoamericana; estudios histórico-sociales*. Jerusalem: Editorial Universitaria Magnes, Universidad Hebrea, pp. 224-233.

937   VIÑAS, Ismael, 1989: 'Los judíos y la sociedad argentina. Un análisis clasista retrospectivo', in Leonardo Senkman, ed., *El antisemitismo en la Argentina*. Buenos Aires: Centro Editor de América Latina, pp. 329-391.

938   WAISMAN, Carlos H., 1987: 'Capitalism, socialism, and the Jews: the view from *Cabildo*', in Judith Laikin Elkin and Gilbert W. Merkx, eds., *The Jewish presence in Latin America*. Boston: Allen and Unwin, pp. 233-254.

939   WAISMAN, Carlos H., 1989: 'La ideología del nacionalismo de derecha en Argentina: el capitalismo, el socialismo y los judíos', in Leonardo Senkman, ed., *El antisemitismo en la Argentina*. Buenos Aires: Centro Editor de América Latina, pp. 209-234.

940   WEISBROT, Robert, 1979: *The Jews of Argentina: from the inquisition to Perón*. Philadelphia: The Jewish Publishing Society of America, 348 pp.

941   WINSBERG, Morton, 1964: *Colonia Baron Hirsch: a Jewish agricultural colony in Argentina*. Gainesville: University of Florida Monographs (Social Sciences, no. 11), 71 pp.

942   WINSBERG, Morton, 1968: 'Jewish agricultural colonization in Entre Rios. Some social and economic aspects of a venture in resettlement', *AJES*, 27/3.

943   WOLFF, Martha, and Myrtha SCHALOM, 1988: *Judíos y argentinos: judíos argentinos*. Buenos Aires: Manrique Zago.

See also: 40; 71; 472; 473; 480; 485; 1022

Bolivia

944   CÍRCULO ISRAELITA, 1987: *Medio siglo de vida judía en La Paz*. La

Paz: Círculo Israelita, 325 pp.

945   KNUDSON, Jerry, 1970: 'The Bolivian immigration bill of 1942: a case study in Latin American anti-semitism', *AJA*, 22/2, pp. 138-58.

946   SEELISCH, Winifred, 1989: 'Jüdische Emigration nach Bolivien Ende der 30er Jahre', in Achim Schrader and Karl Heinrich Rengstorf, eds., *Europäische Juden in Lateinamerika*. St. Ingbert: Werner J. Röhrig Verlag, pp. 77-101.

See also: 497

Brazil

947   ALEXANDER, Frida, 1967: *Filipson: memórias da primeira colônia judaica no Rio Grande do Sul*. São Paulo: Editôra Fulger, 237 pp.

948   BLAY, Eva Alterman, 1989: 'Inquisition, Inquistionen. Aspekte der Teilhabe der Juden am sozio-politischen Leben im Brasilien der 30er Jahre', in Achim Schrader and Karl Heinrich Rengstorf, eds., *Europäische Juden in Lateinamerika*. St. Ingbert: Werner J. Röhrig Verlag, pp. 435-470.

949   BREUNIG, Bernd, 1983: *Die Deutsche Rolandwanderung*. München: Nymphenburger, 291 pp.

950   BREUNIG, Bernd, 1989: 'Der Beitrag der deutschen Juden zur ländlichen Kolonisation Nord-Paranás im Rahmen der Rolandwanderung 1932-1938', in Achim Schrader and Karl Heinrich Rengstorf, eds., *Europäische Juden in Lateinamerika*. St. Ingbert: Werner J. Röhrig Verlag, pp. 138-156.

951   CARNEIRO, Maria Luiza Tucci, 1988: *O anti-semitismo na era Vargas: fantasmas de uma geração (1930-1945)*. São Paulo: Editora Brasiliense, 512 pp.

952   COHEN, Vera Regina de Aquino, 1980: 'A imigração judaica no Rio Grande do Sul', in Aldair Marli Lando, ed., *RS: Imigração e colonização no Rio Grande do Sul*. Porto Alegre: Mercado Aberto, pp. 195-233.

953   EIZIRIK, Moysés, 1984: *Aspectos da vida judaica no Rio Grande do Sul*. Caxias do Sul: Editora da Universidade de Caxias do Sul and Porto Alegre: Escola Superior de Teologia São Lourenço de Brindes, pp. 184.

954   EIZIRIK, Moysés, 1986: *Imigrantes judeus: relatos, crônicas e perfis*. Caxias do Sul: Editora da Universidade de Caxias do Sul and Porto Alegre: Escola Superior de Teologia e Espiritualidade Franciscana, 136 pp.

955   FALBEL, Nachman, 1986: 'Early Zionism in Brazil: the founding years, 1913-1922', *AJA*, 38/2, pp. 123-136.

956   KOSMINSKY, Ethel Volfzon, 1985: *Rolândia, a terra prometida: judeus refugiados do nazismo no norte do Paraná*. São Paulo: Centro de Estudos Judaicos, Universidade de São Paulo, 149 pp.

957   KOSMINSKY, Ethel Volfzon, 1989: 'Rolândia, a terra prometida: judeus refugiados do nazismo no norte do Paraná', *EML*, no. 11, pp. 97-110.

958   KOSMINSKY, Ethel Volfzon, 1989: 'Rolândia - Das verheißene Land. Juden auf der Flucht vor dem Nationalsozialismus im Norden von Paraná/Brasilien', in Achim Schrader and Karl Heinrich Rengstorf, eds., *Europäische Juden in Lateinamerika*. St. Ingbert: Werner J. Röhrig Verlag, pp. 123-137.

959   KRAUSZ, Rosa, 1982: 'Some aspects of intermarriage in the Jewish community of São Paulo, Brazil', *AJA*, 34/2, pp. 216-230.

960   LARGMAN, Esther and Robert M. LEVINE, 1986: 'Jews in the tropics: Bahian Jews in the early twentieth century', *AM*, 43/2, pp. 159-170.

961   LESSER, Jeff H., 1988: 'Continuity and change within an immigrant community: the Jews of São Paulo, 1924-1945', *LBR*, 25/2, pp. 45-58.

962   LESSER, Jeff H., 1989: 'Diferencias regionales en el desarrollo histórico de las comunidades judeo-brasileñas contemporáneas: San Pablo y Porto Alegre', *EML*, no. 11, pp. 71-84.

963   LESSER, Jeff, H., 1989: 'Historische Entwicklung und regionale Unterschiede der zeitgenössischen brasilianisch-jüdischen Gemeinden', in Achim Schrader and Karl Heinrich Rengstorf, eds., *Europäische Juden in Lateinamerika*. St. Ingbert: Werner J. Röhrig Verlag, pp. 361-377.

964   LEVINE, Robert M., 1968: 'Brazil's Jews during the Vargas era and after', *LBR*, 2/5, pp. 45-58.

965   MAIER, Max Hermann, 1975: *Ein Frankfurter Rechtsanwalt wird Kaffeepflanzer im Urwald Brasiliens: Bericht eines Emigranten 1938-1975*. Frankfurt: Josef Knecht, 143 pp.

966   NACHMAN, Falbel, 1984: *Estudo sobre a comunidade judaica no Brasil*. São Paulo: Federação Israelita do Estado do São Paulo, 197 pp.

967   NEVES, Clarissa Baeta, 1989: 'Die Integration der Juden in das südbrasilianische Wirtschaftssystem', in Achim Schrader and Karl Heinrich Rengstorf, eds., *Europäische Juden in Lateinamerika*. St. Ingbert: Werner

J. Röhrig Verlag, pp. 321-343.

968 NICOLAIEWSKY, Eva, 1975: *Os Israelitas no Rio Grande do Sul*. Porto Alegre: Editora Garatuja, 108 pp.

969 NIXDORF, Oswaldo, 1979: *Pionier im brasilianischen Urwald. Die abenteuerreiche Geschichte der deutschen Siedlung Rolândia*. Tübingen: Horst Erdmann Verlag, 319 pp.

970 PINKUSS, Fritz, 1974: 'Um ensaio acerca da imigração judaica no Brasil após o cataclisma de 1937 e da Segunda Guerra Mundial', *RH/SP*, 50/2, pp. 599-607.

971 RATTNER, Henrique, 1977: *Tradição e mudança: (a comunidade judaica em São Paulo)*. São Paulo: Editora Atica, 198 pp.

972 RATTNER, Henrique, 1987: 'Economic and social mobility of Jews in Brazil', in Judith Laikin Elkin and Gilbert W. Merkx, eds., *The Jewish presence in Latin America*. Boston: Allen and Unwin, pp. 187-200.

973 RATTNER, Henrique, 1989: 'Jude sein und Brasilianer. Sozial-kulturelle Identitätsprobleme in Brasilien', in Achim Schrader and Karl Heinrich Rengstorf, eds., *Europäische Juden in Lateinamerika*. St. Ingbert: Werner J. Röhrig Verlag, pp. 344-358.

974 SCHWEIDSON, Jacques, 1985: *Judeus de bombachas e chimarrão*. Rio de Janeiro: José Olympio, 413 pp.

975 TRENTO, Angelo, 1989: 'Die jüdische Immigration nach Brasilien nach Erlaß der Rassengesetze: die Colônia Mussolini', in Achim Schrader and Karl Heinrich Rengstorf, eds., *Europäische Juden in Lateinamerika*. St. Ingbert: Werner J. Röhrig Verlag, pp. 102-120.

976 VIERA, Nelson, 1988: 'Símbolos judíos de resistencia en la literatura brasileña moderna', in *Judaica latinoamericana; estudios histórico-sociales*. Jerusalem: Editorial Universitaria Magnes, Universidad Hebrea, pp. 234-247.

977 VILLANUEVA, Orion, 1974: *Rolândia: terra de pioneiros*. Londrina: Gráfica Ipê, 249 pp.

978 WOLFF, Egon and Frieda WOLFF, 1975: *Os judeus no Brasil imperial: uma pesquisa nos documentos e no noticiário carioca da época*. São Paulo: Centro de Estudos Judaicos, Universidade de São Paulo, 549 pp.

979 WOLFF, Egon and Frieda WOLFF, 1979: *Judeus nos primórdios do Brasil-República visto especialmente pela documentação no Rio de Janeiro*.

Rio de Janeiro: Edição da Biblioteca Israelita H.N. Bialik, 297 pp.

See also: 916

Chile

980   BÖHM, Günter, 1982: 'Inmigración judía a Chile durante el siglo XIX', *RCH*, no. 1, pp. 69-76.

981   BÖHM, Günter, 1988: 'Inmigración de judíos de habla alemana a Chile y Perú durante el siglo XIX', *JGSWGL*, vol. 25, pp. 455-493.

982   BÖHM, Günter, 1988: 'La vida judía en Chile y en Perú durante el siglo XIX', in *Judaica latinoamericana; estudios histórico-sociales*. Jerusalem: Editorial Universitaria Magnes, Universidad Hebrea, pp. 32-40.

983   NES-EL, Moshe, 1984: *Historia de la comunidad israelita sefardí de Chile*. Santiago: Editorial Nascimento, 385 pp.

984   NES-EL, Moshe, 1986: *La inmigración judía a Chile en la época del Holocausto*. Tel Aviv: Instituto Israelí Chileno de Cultura, 20 pp.

985   NES-EL, Moshe, 1988: 'Natalio Berman: un líder sionista en Chile', in *Judaica latinoamericana; estudios histórico-sociales*. Jerusalem: Editorial Universitaria Magnes, Universidad Hebrea, pp. 167-173.

Colombia

986   NEUMANN, Gerhard, 1941: 'German Jews in Colombia: a study in immigrant adjustment', *JSS*, 3, pp. 387-398.

987   ROSENTHAL, Celia, 1956: 'The Jews of Barranquilla: a study of a Jewish community in South America', *JSS*, 18, pp. 262-274.

988   SMITH, J.K., 1962: 'Jewish education in Barranquilla: assimilation versus group survival', *JSS*, 35/3-4, pp. 239-254.

989   TOLIVER, Suzanne Shipley, 1987: 'In exile: the Latin American diaries of Katja Hayek Arendt', *AJA*, 39/2, pp. 157-188.

990   TWINAM, Ann, 1980: 'From Jew to Basque: ethnic myths and Antioqueño entrepreneurship', *JIASWA*, 22/1, pp. 81-107.

Costa Rica

991   GUDMUNDSON, Lowell, 1987: 'Costa Rica Jewry: an economic and political outline', in Judith Laikin Elkin and Gilbert W. Merkx, eds., *The Jewish presence in Latin America*. Boston: Allen and Unwin, pp. 219-232.

992   SCHIFTER SIKORA, Jacobo and Mario SOLERA CASTRO, 1979: *El mundo judío en Costa Rica (1900-1950)*. Heredia: Universidad Nacional "Campus Omar Dengo", Instituto de Estudios Latinoamericanos, 222 pp.

993   SCHIFTER SIKORA, Jacobo, Lowell GUDMUNDSON and Mario SOLERA CASTRO, 1979: *El judío en Costa Rica*. San José: Editorial Universidad Estatal a Distancia, 385 pp.

Cuba

994   BEJARANO, Margalit, 1988: 'The deproletarization of Cuban Jewry', in *Judaica latinoamericana: estudios histórico-sociales*. Jerusalem: Editorial Universitaria Magnes, Universidad Hebrea, pp. 57-67.

995   GELLMAN, Irwin, 1971-2: 'The St. Louis tragedy', *AJHQ*, vol. 61, pp. 144-156.

996   HERLIN, Hans, 1985: *Die Reise der Verdammten. Die Tragödie der St. Louis*. Frankfurt and Vienna: Ullstein Sachbuch, 182 pp.

997   KONOVITCH, Barry J., 1989-90: 'The fiftieth anniversary of the St Louis: what really happened', *AJH*, 79/2, pp. 203-209.

998   LIEBMAN, Seymour B., 1970: 'The Cuban Jewish community in south Florida', *AJYB*, vol. 71, pp. 238-246.

999   MENDELSOHN, John, 1982: *Jewish emigration: the S.S. St. Louis affair and other cases*. New York: Garland, 270 pp.

1000   SAPIR, Boris, 1946: 'Jews in Cuba', *JR*, 5 (July/Sept), pp. 109-144.

1001   SAPIR, Boris, 1947: 'Jewish organizations in Cuba', *JR*, 4 (Jan-March), pp. 263-281.

1002   SAPIR, Boris, 1948: *The Jewish community of Cuba*. New York: J.T.S.P. University Press (Jewish Life in the Americas Series, no. 3), 94 pp.

1003   THOMAS, Gordon and Max MORGAN-WITTS, 1974: *Voyage of the damned*. London: Hodder and Stoughton, 317 pp.

Dominican Republic

1004   BURLEY, Nancy and Richard SYMANSKI, 1973: 'The Jewish colony of Sosúa', *AAAG*, 63/3, pp. 366-378.

1005   EICHEN, Joseph D., 1980: *Sosúa: una colonia hebrea en la República Dominicana*. Santiago (DR): Universidad Católica Madre y Maestra, 125 pp.

1006   KÄTSCH, S., E.M. KÄTSCH and H.P. DAVID, 1970: *Sosúa: Verheißenes Land: Eine Dokumentation zu Adoptionsproblemen deutsch-jüdischer Siedler der Dominikanischen Republik*. Dortmund, 197 pp.

1007   SCHOENHALS, Kai P., 1985: 'An extraordinary migration: Jews in the Dominican Republic', *CR*, 14/4, pp. 17.

See: 138; 139; 141

Haiti

See also: 1162

Mexico

1008   BANKIER, David, 1986: 'El movimiento Alemania Libre y la comunidad judía de México', in *Ninth World Congress of Jewish Studies (Jerusalem, Aug. 4-12, 1985), Div. B, vol. 3*. Jerusalem: World Congress of Jewish Studies, pp. 329-336.

1009   BOPP, Marianne O. de, 1983: 'The Jewish exile-intelligentsia in Latin America as exemplified by Mexico', in Hans-Bernhard Moeller, ed., *Latin America and the literature of exile*. Heidelberg: Carl Winter Universitäts-verlag, pp. 113-136.

1010   GOJMAN DE BACKAL, Alicia, 1988: 'Minorías, estado y movimiento nacionalistas de la clase media en México: Liga Anti-China y Anti-Judía (siglo XX)', in *Judaica latinoamericana: estudios histórico-sociales*. Jerusalem: Editorial Universitaria Magnes, Universidad Hebrea, pp. 174-191.

1011   GOJMAN DE BACKAL, Alicia, 1989: 'Deutsche Beteiligung an der Bewegung der "Goldhemden" im Mexiko der 30er Jahre', in Achim Schrader and Karl Heinrich Rengstorf, eds., *Europäische Juden in Lateinamerika*. St. Ingbert: Werner J. Röhrig Verlag, pp. 425-434.

1012   KALMAR, Stephen, 1987: *Goodbye Vienna!* San Francisco: Strawberry Hill Press, 251 pp.

1013   KRAUSE, Corinne Azen, 1970: *The Jews in Mexico: a history with special emphasis on the period from 1857-1930.* PhD Thesis, University of Pittsburgh.

1014   KRAUSE, Corinne Azen, 1971/2: 'Mexico: another promised land? A review of projects for Jewish colonization in Mexico: 1881-1925', *AJHQ*, 61/1-4, pp. 325-341.

1015   LEPKOWSKI, Tadeusz, 1983: 'Pequeños empresarios judío-polacos en México (1918-1930)', in *Capitales, empresarios y obreros europeos en América Latina (Actas del 6° Congreso de AHILA, Stockholm, 25-28 de Mayo 1981).* Stockholm: Instituto de Estudios Latinoamericanos (monografías, no. 8, vol. 2), pp. 493-500.

1016   LESSER, Harriet Sara, 1972: *A history of the Jewish community of Mexico City, 1912-1970.* PhD Thesis, Jewish Theological Seminary and Columbia University.

1017   MODENA, Maria Eugenia, 1982: *Pasaporte de culturas: viaje por la vida de un judío ruso en México.* México, DF: Instituto Nacional de Antropología e Historia, 109 pp.

1018   POHLE, Fritz, 1989: 'Alemania libre y sionismo. Política de alianza de los exiliados comunistas hacia la emigración judía', *EML*, no. 11, pp. 61-70.

1019   SCHECHNER, Tzvi, 1988: '"Kehile": un concepto común heredado en México y Argentina', in *Judaica latinoamericana: estudios histórico-sociales.* Jerusalem: Editorial Universitaria Magnes, Universidad Hebrea, pp. 115-128.

1020   SELIGSON, Silvia, 1983: *Los judíos en México: un estudio preliminar.* México, DF: Centro de Investigaciones y Estudios Superiores en Antropología Social (Cuadernos de la Casa Chata, no. 88), 200 pp.

1021   SOURASKY, León, 1965: *Historia de la comunidad israelita de México, 1917-1942.* México, DF: Imprenta Moderna Pimentel, 291 pp.

1022   ZADOFF, Efraim, 1986: 'Jewish education systems in Mexico and Argentina (1935-1955): a comparative view', in *Ninth World Congress of Jewish Studies (Jerusalem, Aug. 4-12, 1985), Div. B, vol. 3.* Jerusalem: World Congress of Jewish Studies, pp. 249-256.

1023   ZADOFF, Efraim, 1988: 'Un análisis comparativo de las redes educativas judías de México y Argentina, 1935-1955', in *Judaica latinoamericana:*

estudios histórico-sociales. Jerusalem: Editorial Universitaria Magnes, Universidad Hebrea, pp. 129-148.

1024   ZÁRATE MIGUEL, Guadalupe, 1986: *México y la diáspora judía.* México, DF: Instituto Nacional de Antropología e Historia, 189 pp.

See also: 588; 593

Nicaragua

1025   MURAVCHIK, Josua, Susan ALBERTS and Antony KORENSTEIN, 1986: 'Sandinista anti-semitism and its apologists', *CT*, 82/3, pp. 25-29.

Panama

1026   FIDANQUE, E. Alvin et al, 1977: *Kol Shearith Israel: cien años de vida judía en Panamá 1876-1976. Kol Shearith Israel: a hundred years of Jewish life in Panama.* Panamá: Congregation Kol Shearith Israel, 487 pp.

1027   KLEPFISZ, Heszel, 1973: 'La población hebrea en la República de Panamá', *RL*, 206, p. 31-42.

1028   SASSO, Dennis C., 1976: 'One century of Jewish life in Panama', *RE*, vol. 42 (Sept.), pp. 18-24.

See also: 598; 599

Paraguay

1029   SEIFERHELD, Alfredo M., 1981: 'Inmigración y presencia judías en el Paraguay', *EP*, 9-10/2-1, 228 pp.

1030   SEIFERHELD, Alfredo M., 1982: 'Los judíos en el Paraguay', *EP*, 10/2, pp. 183-258.

1031   SEIFERHELD, Alfredo M., 1984: *Los judíos en el Paraguay. Vol. 1: inmigración y presencia judía (siglo XVI-1935).* Asunción: El Lector, 228 pp.

Peru

1032   BÖHM, Günter, 1985: *Judíos en el Perú durante el siglo XIX.* Santiago de Chile: Universidad de Chile, 184 pp.

1033   TRAHTEMBERG SIEDERER, León, 1987: *La inmigración judía al Perú, 1848-1948: Una historia documentada de la inmigración de los judíos de habla alemana.* Lima: Asociación Judía de Beneficencia y Culto de 1870, 322 pp.

See also: 982

Uruguay

1034   AVNI, Haim and Rosa Perla RAICHER, 1986: *Memorias del Uruguay: Holocausto y lucha por la fundación del Estado de Israel.* Jerusalem: Institute of Contemporary Judaism (Oral History Division), Hebrew University of Jerusalem, 111 pp.

1035   FELDMAN, Miguel, 1988: 'Inmigrantes y antisemitas en el Uruguay de hace 50 años', *CX*, verano.

1036   NEMIROVSKY, Israel, 1987: *Albores del judaísmo en el Uruguay.* Montevideo, 288 pp.

1037   OXMAN, Ramón, 1987: *La Colonia 19 de Abril: una experiencia de colonización agraria judía en el Uruguay.* Montevideo: Ed. del Nuevo Mundo, 68 pp.

1038   PORZECANSKI, Teresa, 1986: *Historias de vida de inmigrantes judíos al Uruguay.* Montevideo: Comunidad Israelita del Uruguay, 243 pp.

1039   RAICHER, Rosa Perla, 1986: 'Asylum in Uruguay for Jewish refugees persecuted by Nazism', in *Ninth World Congress of Jewish Studies (Jerusalem, Aug. 4-12, 1985), Div. B, vol. 3.* Jerusalem: World Congress of Jewish Studies, pp. 221-224.

1040   RAICHER, Rosa Perla, 1988: 'Asilo en el Uruguay de refugiados judíos perseguidos por el nazismo', in *Judaica latinoamericana: estudios histórico-sociales.* Jerusalem: Editorial Universitaria Magnes, Universidad Hebrea, pp. 68-78.

See also: 879

Venezuela

1041   AIZENBERG, Isidoro, 1978: 'Los intentos de establecer un cementerio judío en el Caracas del siglo XIX', *BH*, 47, pp. 243- 254.

1042   AIZENBERG, Isidoro, 1983: 'The 1855 expulsion of the Curaçaoan Jews from Coro, Venezuela', *AJH*, 72/4, pp. 495-507.

1043   AIZENBERG, Isidoro, 1983: *La comunidad judía de Coro, 1824-1900: una historia*. Caracas, 244 pp.

1044   EMMANUEL, Isaac S., 1973: *The Jews of Coro, Venezuela*. Cincinatti: American Jewish Archives, 63 pp.

1045   FORTIQUE, José Rafael, 1973: *Los motines anti-judíos de Coro*. Maracaibo: Editorial Puente, 91 pp.

1046   NASSÍ, Mario, 1981: *La comunidad ashkenazi de Caracas: breve historia institucional*. Caracas: La Union Israelita de Caracas, 78 pp.

1047   OSTFELD, Klara, 1986: *Luz y sombra de mi vida: memorias*. Caracas: Editorial Arte, 467 pp.

LATVIAN

Bibliography

1048   TĀLE, Gunita, 1990: *Latvieši Latīnamerikā: literatūras saraksts. Latvians in Latin America: List of publications.* Riga: Letonikas nodaļa, Latvijas Valsts bibliotēka [Riga: State Library of Latvia, Lettonics Department], mimeo., 39 pp.

General

1049   KRASNAIS, Vilberts, 1980: *Latviešu kolōnijas.* Melbourne: Kārļa Zariņa fonds, Melbourne [reprint of 1938 edition], 540 pp.

Brazil

1050   AUGELLI, J., 1958: 'The Latvians of Varpa: a foreign colony on the Brazilian pioneer fringe', *GR*, vol. 48, pp. 365-87.

1051   BRŪVERS, Arnold, 1970: *Latvieši palmu zemē.* Rio de Janeiro, 89 pp.

1052   TUPES, Milia, 1979: *Contribução ao estudo da colonização no estado de São Paulo. Ensaio sobre a Côlonia Varpa.* São Paulo: Coleção Museu Paulista (Série de História, vol. 8), 122 pp.

LITHUANIAN

General

1053   EIDINTAS, Alfonsas, 1985: 'The emigration policy of the Tautininkai regime in Lithuania, 1926-1940', *JBS*, 16/11, pp. 64-72.

1054   EIDINTAS, Alfonsas, 1989: *Litovskaia emigracija v strany Severnoj i Južnoj Ameriki v 1868-1940 g.g.* Vilnius: Mokslas, 217 pp.

1055   MICHELSONAS, S., 1961: *Lietuvių išeivija Amerikoje, 1868-1961.* Boston: Keleivis, 499 pp.

1056   ZOKAS, A., 1972: *Nuo Dubysos iki la Platos: Atsiminimai.* Vilnius: Vaga, 264 pp.

Argentina

1057   BRIZGYS, Jurgis, ed., 1963: *Lietuviai Argentinoj.*   Rosario: Lietuvių bendrumenes leidinys, 80 pp.

1058   BRIZGYS, Jurgis, 1968: *Lietuvos laisves kovos metai, 1918-1968.* Rosario: Lietuvių bendrumenes leidinys, 213 pp.

1059   MIKELIONIS, Juozas, 1954: *Benamiai.* Buenos Aires, 215 pp.

1060   MIZARA-RASODA, R., 1928: *Argentina ir ten gyvenantieji lietuviai.* Brooklyn: Amerikos lietuvių darbininkų literatūros d-ja, 189 pp.

Brazil

1061   DANGELA, Juozas, 1933: *Lietuviai Brazilijoje.* Kaunas: Nepriklausomu rašytoju ir žurnalistu grupes leid., Nr 2, 426 pp.

1062   SAULAITIS, A., ed., 1976: *Lietuvių imigracijos Brazilijon penkiasdešimt-metis, 1926-1976 – Cinquentenario da imigração lituana no Brasil – Red. ir išleido Lietuviu, imigracijos Brazilijon penkiasdešimtmečio k-tas.* São Paulo, 207 pp.

LUXEMBOURGER

Argentina

1063 NILLES, Léon N., 1974: 'San Antonio de Iraola: Luxemburger in der Pampa', *RV*, 30/50. pp. 34-37.

Brazil

1064 FRIEDRICH, Evy, 1983: 'Ein Zinnen schreibt aus Brasilien', *FB*, pp. 42-52.

1065 SPRUNCK, A., 1960: 'L'émigration luxembourgeoise en Amérique méridionale dans la première moitié du 19ᵉ siècle', *LAH*, no. 2, pp. 3-39.

1066 THILL, Robert, 1971: '1921-1971: Luxemburger Pioniere in Brasilien', *AU*, 25, pp. 59-64.

Guatemala

1067 CALMES, Albert, 1960: 'L'émigration luxembourgeoise au Guatémala', *DW*, 13/7.

MALTESE

Argentina

1068   ATTARD, Lawrence E., 1985: *The great exodus (1918-1939)*. Valletta: Publishers Enterprises Group, 141 pp.

Brazil

1069   ATTARD, Lawrence E, 1983: *Men and means: early Maltese emigration (1800-1914)*. Valletta: Gulf Publishing, 58 pp.

MENNONITE

General

1070   BENDER, Harold S., 1939: 'With the Mennonite refugees in Brazil and Paraguay: a personal narrative', *MQR*, vol. 13, pp. 59-70.

1071   REDEKOP, Calvin Wall, 1969: *The Old Colony Mennonites: dilemmas of ethnic minority life.* Baltimore: The Johns Hopkins University Press, 302 pp.

See also: 452

Belize

1072   EVERITT, John C., 1983: 'Mennonites in Belize', *JCG*, 3/2, pp. 82-93.

1073   HALL, Jerry Alan, 1973: *Mennonite agriculture in a tropical environment: an analysis of the development and productivity of a mid-latitude agricultural system in British Honduras.* PhD Thesis, Clark University.

See also: 1084

Bolivia

1074   PEREIRA M., Rene, 1988: *Hacia una política de inmigración extranjera. Análisis de las colonias extranjeras en Bolivia.* La Paz: Consejo Nacional de Población, 33 pp.

1075   WESSEL, K.K. and J.A. WESSEL, 1967: *The Mennonites in Bolivia. An historical and present social-economic evaluation.* Ithaca: Latin American Studies Program, Cornell University.

Brazil

1076   KLASSEN, Peter, 1937: 'The Mennonites of Brazil', *MQR*, vol. 11, pp. 107-118.

1077   KLASSEN, Peter, 1947: 'Mennonites in Brazil', *ML*, 2/1, pp. 37-43.

1078   MINNICH, Reynolds Herbert, 1969: 'Developing democrats: socio-cultural change among the Brazilian Mennonites', in Merrill Rippy, ed., *Cultural change in Brazil*. Muncie, Indiana: Ball State University (papers from the Midwest Association for Latin American Studies), pp. 24-35.

1079   MINNICH, Reynolds Herbert, 1970: *The Mennonite immigrant communities in Paraná, Brazil*. Cuernavaca: Centro Intercultural de Documentación (Sondeos, No. 64), 388 pp.

See also: 1070

Mexico

1080   ACOSTA, Jaime, 1975: 'Hazañas de los Chihuahuanueses rubios', *CO*, vol. 39 (Aug), pp. 352-362.

1081   ALLEN, Gordon and Calvin REDEKOP, 1967: 'Individual differences in survival and reproduction among Old Colony Mennonites in Mexico: progress to October 1966', *EQ*, 14/2, pp. 103-111.

1082   EIGHMY, Jeffrey L., 1989: *Mennonite architecture: diachronic evidence for rapid diffusion in rural communities*. New York: AMS Press, 220 pp.

1083   FRETZ, Joseph W., 1945: *Mennonite colonies in Mexico*. Akron, Pa.: Mennonite Central Committee.

1084   SAWATZKY, H.L., 1971: *They sought a country: Mennonite colonization in Mexico*. Berkeley: University of California Press, 387 pp.

Paraguay

1085   FRETZ, Joseph W., 1953: *Pilgrims in Paraguay*. Scottdale, Pa.: Herald Press, 247 pp.

1086   HACK, Hendrik, 1961: *Die Kolonisation der Mennoniten im paraguayischen Chaco*. Amsterdam: Koenigliches Tropeninstitut Nr. 138 (Abteilung für kulturelle und physische Anthropologie, Nr. 65).

1087   HACK, Hendrik, 1976: *Indianer und Mennoniten im paraguayischen Chaco*. Amsterdam: CEDLA (Incidentele Publicaties, 7), 161 pp.

1088   HACK, Hendrik, 1983: 'Land problems in the Paraguayan Chaco', *BELC*, 34, pp. 99-116

1089   HECHT, Alfred, 1976: 'The agricultural economy of the Mennonite settlers in Paraguay: the impact of a road', *EK*, vol. 42, pp. 42-48.

1090   KRAUSE, Anne-Marie Elizabeth, 1952: *Mennonite settlement in the Paraguayan Chaco*. Chicago: University of Chicago (Department of Geography Research Paper, no. 25), 143 pp.

1091   PLETT, Rudolf, 1979: *Presencia Menonita en el Paraguay: origen, doctrina, estructura y funcionamiento*. Asunción: Instituto Bíblico Asunción, 156 pp.

1092   RAMÍREZ RUSSO, Manfredo, 1983: *El Chaco Paraguayo: integración de los menonitas a la sociedad nacional*. Asunción: Editorial El Foro, 377 pp.

1093   REDEKOP, Calvin, 1980: *Strangers become neighbors: Mennonite and indigenous relations in the Paraguayan Chaco*. Scottdale, Penn. and Kitchener, Ont.: Herald Press, 305 pp.

See also: 153; 155; 1070

NORWEGIAN

General

1094   STANG, Gudmund, 1979: 'La emigración noruega', in *La emigración europea a la América Latina: fuentes y estado de investigación (informes presentados a la IV Reunión de Historiadores Latinoamericanistas Europeos)*. Berlin: Colloquium Verlag (Bibliotheca Ibero-Americana), pp. 104-112.

1095   SUNDT, Hans, 1968: *Innen alt går i glemmeboken. Erindringer av selvopplevelser fra Argentina, Chile og Uruguay*. Oslo: Boksentralen, 156 pp.

See also: 1386; 1387

Argentina

See: 361

Brazil

1096   ISACHSEN, Gunnar, 1937: *Norsk skibsfart på Brasil i feberårene 1891-1893*. Oslo: Norsk sjøfartsmuseum, 25 pp.

Ecuador

1097   HOFF, Stein, 1985: *Drømmen om Galapagos: en ukjent norsk utvandrer-historie*. Oslo: Grøndahl, 211 pp.

POLISH

Bibliographies

1098   SCHNEPF, R. and K. SMOLONA, 1978: *Bibliografia polskiej literatury latynoamerykanistycznej, 1945-1977.* Warsaw.

1099   PACZYŃSKA, Irena and Andrzej PILCH, 1979: *Materiały do bibliografii dziejów emigracji oraz skupisk polonijnych w Ameryce północnej i południowej w XIX i XX wieku.* Warsaw.

General

1100   DOBOSIEWICZ, Zbigniew and Waldemar RÓMMEL, eds., 1977: *Polonia w Ameryce Łacińskiej.* Lublin: Wydawnictwo Lubelskie, 248 pp.

1101   GRONIOWSKI, Krzysztof, 1976: 'The main stages in the history of Polish immigrants in South America', *PWA*, 17/1-2, pp. 152-160.

1102   GRONIOWSKI, Krzysztof, 1979: 'A emigração polonesa para a América Latina nos séculos XIX e XX. As fontes históricas e o estado de estudos', in *La emigración europea a la América Latina: fuentes y estado de investigación (informes presentados a la IV Reunión de Historiadores Latinamericanistas Europeos).* Berlin: Colloquium Verlag (Bibliotheca Ibero-Americana), pp. 241-256.

1103   LERNER, Harold, 1962: *The role of the Poles in the development of Latin American civilization.* PhD Thesis, New York University.

1104   ŁEPKOWSKI, Tadeusz, 1978: 'La presencia de la emigración polaca en América Latina y la política cultural de Polonia en este continente', *EL*, no. 4, pp. 221-232.

1105   PARADOWSKA, Maria, 1977: *Polacy w Ameryce Południowej.* Wrocław: Ossolineum, 316 pp.

1106   PARADOWSKA, Maria, 1984: *Podróżnicy i emigranci.* Szkice z dziejów polskiego wychodźstwa w Ameryce Południowej. Warsaw: Interpress, 220 pp.

1107   PYZIK, E., 1966: *Los polacos en la República Argentina y América del Sur desde el año 1812.* Buenos Aires: Comité de Homenaje al Milenio de Polonia, 230 pp.

See also: 341; 461; 1419

Central America

1108   ŁEPKOWSKI, Tadeusz, 1983: 'Polonia w krajach Ameryki Centralnej', in Marcin Kula, ed., *Dzieje Polonii w Ameryce Łacińskiej.* Wrocław: Polska Akademia Nauk, pp. 112-127.

1109   PARADOWSKA, Maria, 1983: 'Los polacos en México y América Central y sus trabajos etnográficos', *EPO*, vol. 9, pp. 183-206.

1110   PARADOWSKA, Maria, 1985: *Polacy w Meksyku i Ameryce Środkowej.* Wrocław: Ossolineum, 383 pp.

Argentina

1111   GLEMP, Józef, 1986: *Kościół i Polonia. Wizyta duszpasterska w Brazylii i Argentynie 1984.* Poznań: Pallotinum, 321 pp.

1112   KLARNER-KOSIŃSKA, Izabela 1983: 'Polonia w Buenos Aires', in Marcin Kula, ed., *Dzieje Polonii w Ameryce Łacińskiej.* Wrocław: Polska Akademia Nauk, pp. 218-245.

1113   ŁUKASZ, Danuta, 1981: 'Las asociaciones polacas en Misiones, 1898-1938', *EL*, no. 8, pp. 169-188.

1114   ŁUKASZ, Danuta, 1983: 'La enseñanza polaca en Misiones 1900-1938', *LS*, vol. 12, pp. 193-219.

1115   ŁUKASZ, Danuta and Ryszard STEMPLOWSKI, 1983: 'Polskie osadnictwo chłopskie w argentyńskim Misiones od końca XIX w do lat trzydziestych XX w', in Marcin Kula, ed., *Dzieje Polonii w Ameryce Łacinskiej.* Wrocław: Polska Akademia Nauk, pp. 246-308.

1116   SMOLANA, Krzysztof, 1983: 'Polonia w Argentynie. Rys historyczny', in Marcin Kula, ed., *Dzieje Polonii w Ameryce Łacińskiej.* Wrocław: Polska Akademia Nauk, pp. 215-217.

1117   STALISZEWSKI, J.E., 1975: *Polish frontier settlement in Misiones, Argentina: formation of the Slavic cultural landscape in Misiones.* PhD Thesis, Columbia University.

1118   STEMPLOWSKI, Ryszard, 1982: 'Los eslavos en Misiones. Consideraciones en torno al número y la distribución geográfica de los campesinos polacos y ucranianos (1897-1938)', *JGSWGL*, vol. 19, pp. 320-390.

1119   STEMPLOWSKI, Ryszard, 1983: 'Los aspectos ecónomicos de los comienzos de la colonización agrícola de los eslavos en Misiones (Argentina) 1897-1903', *LS*, vol. 12, pp. 129-153.

See also: 341; 1107; 1420; 1421; 1422

Bolivia

1120   KLARNER-KOSIŃSKA, Izabela 1983: 'Polonia w Boliwii', in Marcin Kula, ed., *Dzieje Polonii w Ameryce Łacińskiej*. Wrocław: Polska Akademia Nauk, pp. 202-205.

Brazil

1121   ANUSZEWSKA, Ewa, 1983: 'Gospodarowanie Polonii brazylijskiej', in Marcin Kula, ed., *Dzieje Polonii w Ameryce Łacińskiej*. Wrocław: Polska Akademia Nauk, pp. 358-378.

1122   ASSORODOBRAJ-KULA, Nina, Witold KULA and Marcin KULA, 1986: *Writing home: immigrants in Brazil and the United States, 1890-1891* (edited and translated by Josephine Wulich). Boulder: East European Monographs, 698 pp.

1123   BARRETO, Maria Theresa Sobierajski, 1983: *Poloneses em Santa Catarina: a colonização do Alto Vale do Rio Tijucas*. Florianópolis: Editora da Universidade Federal de Santa Catarina and Editora Lunardelli, 143 pp.

1124   DWORECKI, Tadeusz, 1980: *Zmagania Polonijne w Brazylii: Polscy Werbiści 1900-1978*. Warsaw: Akademia Teologii Katolickiej, 840 pp.

1125   FOUNTAIN, Anne, 1988: 'Promises, promises: Polish immigration to Brazil, 1871-1939', *SAN*, vol. 19, pp. 29-36.

1126   GARDOLINSKI, Edmundo, 1977: *Escolas da colonização polonesa no Rio Grande do Sul*. Caxias do Sul: Escola Superior de Teologia and Porto Alegre: Universidade de Caxias do Sul, 136 pp.

1127   GRONIOWSKI, Krzysztof, 1972: *Polska emigracja zarobkowa w Brazlii, 1871-1914*. Warsaw: Polska Akademia Nauk (Instytut Historii), 295 pp.

1128   GRONIOWSKI, Krzysztof, 1980: 'O mito da América Latina no campo polonês no período das "febres brasileiras"', *EL*, no. 6, pt. 1, pp. 105-124.

1129   IANNI, Octavio, 1960: 'Do polonês ao polaco', *RMP*, nova série, vol. 12.

1130   IANNI, Octavio, 1961: 'A situação social do polonês em Curitiba', *SA*, December, pp. 375-388.

1131   IGNATOWICZ, Maria Anna, 1983: 'Przemiany społeczności polskiej w Brazylii', in Marcin Kula, ed., *Dzieje Polonii w Ameryce Łacińskiej*. Wrocław: Polska Akademia Nauk, pp. 379-410.

1132   KLARNER, Izabela, 1975: *Emigracja z Królestwa Polskiego do Brazylii 1890-1914*. Warsaw: Książka i Wiedza, 167 pp.

1133   KLARNER, Izabela, 1983: 'Polonia w São Paulo', in Marcin Kula, ed., *3zieje Polonii w Ameryce Łacińskiej*. Wrocław: Polska Akademia Nauk, pp. 322-357.

1134   KOREYWO-RYBCZYŃSKA, Maria Teresa, 1983: 'Polityka Polski wobec emigracji w Ameryce Łacińskiej. Od mirażu ekspansji do polityki współpracy', in Marcin Kula, ed., *Dzieje Polonii w Ameryce Łacińskiej*. Wrocław: Polska Akademia Nauk, pp. 443-480.

1135   KRASICKI, Marek, 1983: 'Sytuacja Polonii brazylijskiej w dobie ustaw nacjonalistycznych prezydenta Getúlio Vargas', in Marcin Kula, ed., *Dzieje Polonii w Ameryce Łacińskiej*. Wrocław: Polska Akademia Nauk, pp. 411-442.

1136   KULA, Marcin, 1976: 'El Brasil y la Polonia de fines de siglo XIX en las cartas de los campesinos emigrados', *JGSWGL*, vol. 13, pp. 38-55.

1137   KULA, Marcin, 1981: *Polonia brazylijska*. Warsaw: Ludowa Spółdzielnia Wydawnicza, 232 pp.

1138   LASOCKI, Stanislas George, 1967: *Participation in nation-building: Polish immigration to Brazil*. PhD Thesis, Claremont University.

1139   MAGALINSKI, Jan, 1980: *Deslocados de guerra em Goiás: imigrantes poloneses em Itabraí*. Goiânia: Editora Universidade Federal de Goiás, 221 pp.

1140   PRICE, Paul H., 1950-51: *The Polish immigrant in Brazil: a study of immigration, assimilation and acculturation*. PhD Thesis, Vanderbilt University.

1141   PRICE, Paul H., 1952: 'The demographic aspects of the Polish migration to Brazil', *IAEA*, 5/4, pp. 46-58.

1142   ROKUSKI, Bronislau Ostoja, 1976: 'Um século de colonização polonesa no Paraná', *BIHGEP*, vol. 28, pp. 117-158.

1143 SMOLANA, Krzysztof, 1979: 'Sobre a gênese do estereotipo do Polonês na América Latina (caso brasileiro)', *EL*, no. 5, pp. 69-80.

1144 STAWINSKI, A.V., 1976: *Primórdios da imigração polonesa no Rio Grande do Sul (1875-1975)*. Caxias do Sul: Universidade de Caxias do Sul, 255 pp.

1145 STEMPLOWSKI, R., 1976: 'Enlistment in Brazil to the Polish Armed Forces, 1940-1944', *PWA*, 17/1-2, pp. 161-172.

1146 TEMPSKI, Edwino Donato, 1971: 'Poloneses no Paraná', *BIHGEP*, vol. 14, 511 pp.

1147 WACHOWICZ, Ruy C., 1970: 'Conjuntura imigratória polonesa no século XIX', in *CBP*, vol 1, pp. 9-27.

1148 WACHOWICZ, Ruy C., 1970: 'A febre brasileira na imigração polonesa', *CBP*, vol 1, pp. 29-55.

1149 WACHOWICZ, Ruy C., 1976: *Abranches: um estudo de história demográfica*. Curitiba, 84 pp.

1150 WACHOWICZ, Ruy C., 1976: *Orleans: um século de subsistência*. Curitiba: Fundação Cultural Casa Romário Martins, 92 pp.

1151 WACHOWICZ, Ruy C., 1977: *Tomás Coelho: uma comunidade campo-nesa*. Curitiba, 49 pp.

1152 WACHOWICZ, Ruy C., 1981: *O camponês polonês no Brasil*. Curitiba: Fundação Cultural Casa Romário Martins, 149 pp.

1153 WÓJCIK, Władysław, 1963: *Lubliniacy w Brazylii*. Warsaw: Ludowa Spoldzielnia Wydawnicza, 199 pp.

See also: 1111; 1433

Chile

1154 KLARNER-KOSIŃSKA, Izabela 1983: 'Polonia w Chile', in Marcin Kula, ed., *Dzieje Polonii w Ameryce Łacińskiej*. Wrocław: Polska Akademia Nauk, pp. 206-214.

Colombia

1155 KLARNER-KOSIŃSKA, Izabela 1983: 'Polonia w Kolumbii', in Marcin

Kula, ed., *Dzieje Polonii w Ameryce Łacińskiej.* Wrocław: Polska Akademia Nauk, pp. 176-177.

Cuba

1156   KULA, Marcin, 1983: 'El proletariado polaco en Cuba en el período de entre-guerras', in *Capitales, empresarios y obreros europeos en América Latina (Actas del 6° Congreso de AHILA, Stockholm, 25-28 de Mayo 1981).* Stockholm: Instituto de Estudios Latinoamericanos (monografías, no. 8, vol. 1), pp. 358-67.

1157   KULA, Marcin, 1983: 'Polonia na Kubie', in Marcin Kula, ed., *Dzieje Polonii w Ameryce Łacińskiej.* Wrocław: Polska Akademia Nauk, pp. 128-156.

1158   KULA, Marcin, 1989: 'Those who failed to reach the United States: Polish proletarians in Cuba during the interwar period', *PAS*, 46/1, pp. 19-41.

Ecuador

1159   KLARNER-KOSIŃSKA, Izabela 1983: 'Polonia w Ekwadorze', in Marcin Kula, ed., *Dzieje Polonii w Ameryce Łacińskiej.* Wrocław: Polska Akademia Nauk, pp. 178-180.

Haiti

1160   KLARNER-KOSIŃSKA, Izabela 1983: 'Polonia w Haiti', in Marcin Kula, ed., *Dzieje Polonii w Ameryce Łacińskiej.* Wrocław: Polska Akademia Nauk, pp. 157-162.

1161   LEPKOWSKI, Tadeusz, 1988: 'Polska obecność w historli Haiti i Haitańczykow. Część I', *PPO*, 14/1, pp. 5-30.

1162   LEPKOWSKI, Tadeusz, 1988: 'Polska obecność w historli Haiti i Haitanczykow. Czesc II', *PPO*, 14/2, pp. 21-40.

1163   LEPKOWSKI, Tadeusz, 1988: 'La présence polonaise dans l'histoire d'Haïti et des Haïtiens', *EL*, no. 11, pp. 141-195.

1164   ST.-JUSTE, Laurore and Enel CLÉRISMÉ, 1983: *Présence polonaise en Haïti.* Port au Prince, 57 pp.

Mexico

1165   ŁEPKOWSKI, Tadeusz, 1983: 'Polonia meksykańska', in Marcin Kula, ed., *Dzieje Polonii w Ameryce Łacińskiej*. Wrocław: Polska Akademia Nauk, pp. 69-111.

See also: 1109; 1110

Paraguay

1166   KLARNER-KOSIŃSKA, Izabela 1983: 'Polonia w Paragwaju', in Marcin Kula, ed., *Dzieje Polonii w Ameryce Łacińskiej*. Wrocław: Polska Akademia Nauk, pp. 323-331.

See also: 1437

Peru

1167   KLARNER-KOSIŃSKA, Izabela 1983: 'Polonia w Peru', in Marcin Kula, ed., *Dzieje Polonii w Ameryce Łacińskiej*. Wrocław: Polska Akademia Nauk, pp. 181-201.

1168   KOCHANEK, Kazimierz, 1979: *Los polacos en el Perú*. Lima: Editorial Salesiana, 200 pp.

Uruguay

1169   KLARNER-KOSIŃSKA, Izabela 1983: 'Polonia w Urugwaju', in Marcin Kula, ed., *Dzieje Polonii w Ameryce Łacińskiej*. Wrocław: Polska Akademia Nauk, pp. 309-322.

See also: 341

Venezuela

1170   SCHNEPF, Ryszard, 1983: 'Polonia w Wenezueli', in Marcin Kula, ed., *Dzieje Polonii w Ameryce Łacińskiej*. Wrocław: Polska Akademia Nauk, pp. 163-175.

PORTUGUESE

Bibliography

1171   PEREIRA, Arnaldo and Joel SERRÃO, 1979: 'Inventariação das fontes e bibliografia relativas à emigração portuguesa (épocas moderna e contemporânea)', in *La emigración europea a la América Latina: fuentes y estado de investigación (informes presentados a la IV Reunión de Historiadores Latinoamericanistas Europeos)*. Berlin: Colloquium Verlag (Biblioteca Ibero-Americana), pp. 53-62.

General

1172   ALMEIDA, Carlos and António BARRETO, 1974: *Capitalismo e emigração em Portugal*. Lisbon: Prelo Editora, 312 pp.

1173   CABRAL, A.M. Pires, 1985: *A emigração na literatura portuguesa: uma colectânea de textos*. Oporto: Centro de Estudos da Secretaria de Estado das Comunidades Portuguesas, 479 pp.

1174   CARDOSO, Agostinho Gabriel, 1968: *O fenómeno económico-social da emigração madeirense*. Coimbra, 43 pp.

1175   GODINHO, Vitorino Magalhães, 1978: 'L'émigration portugaise (XVe.-XXe. siècles): une constante structurale et les réponses aux changements du monde', *RHES*, no. 1, pp. 5-32.

1176   PEREIRA, Miriam Halpern, 1981: *A política portuguesa de emigração 1850-1930*. Lisbon: A Regra do Jogo, 259 pp.

1177   RIBEIRO, F.G. Cassola, 1983: 'Emigración portuguesa para países de América Latina', in *Migraciones latinas y formación de la nación latinoamericana*. Caracas: Universidad Simón Bolívar, pp. 521-532.

1178   SERRÃO, Joel, 1977, (3rd ed): *A emigração portuguesa: sondagem histórica*. Lisbon: Livros Horizonte.

1179   SILVA, Joaquim Palminha, 1987: *"Comunidades portuguesas" e sua imprensa: subsídios para um inventário*. Oporto: Centro de Estudos da Secretaria de Estado das Comunidades Portuguesas, 73 pp.

Argentina

1180 BORGES, Marcelo J., 1986: 'La inmigración portuguesa en el contexto inmigratorio argentino, 1871-1914', in *Migrare: Revista dos Seminários de Verão*. Lisbon: Secretaria de Estado das Comunidades Portuguesas, 43 pp.

1181 BORGES, Marcelo J., 1989: 'Los portugueses en Buenos Aires a mediados del siglo XIX: una aproximación socio-demográfica', *EML*, no. 12, pp. 353-382.

1182 MASCARUCCI, Paula, 1985: *Monografía sobre el periódico "Ecos de Portugal"*. Oporto: Centro de Estudos da Secretaria de Estado das Comunidades Portuguesas, 87 pp.

1183 MENDES PEREIRA, José and José DIAS RATO, 1969: *Historia del Club Portugués de Buenos Aires*. Buenos Aires: Impr. Sur, 221 pp.

Brazil

1184 ALENCASTRO, Luiz Felipe de, 1984: 'Prolétaires et esclaves: immigrés portugais et captifs africains à Rio de Janeiro, 1850-1872', *CRIAR*, no. 4, pp. 119-158.

1185 ARROTEIA, Jorge Carvalho, 1983: *A emigração portuguesa: suas origens e distribuição*. Lisbon: Instituto de Cultura e Língua Portuguesa, 172 pp.

1186 ASSUMPÇÃO, Vera, 1985: *A história exemplar de uma família cafeicultora de origem portuguesa*. Oporto: Centro de Estudos da Secretaria de Estado das Comunidades Portuguesas, 30 pp.

1187 BENIS, Maria Ioannis, 1979: 'A emigração de 1856 à 1875 vista de Viana do Castelo', *RHES*, no. 3, pp. 85-100.

1188 BENIS, Maria Ioannis, 1981: 'Uma contra-imagem do Brasileiro', *RHES*, no. 7, pp. 129-137.

1189 BRITO, Raquel Soeiro de, 1960: *Agricultores e pescadores portugueses na cidade do Rio de Janeiro*. Lisbon: Imprensa Nacional.

1190 CAMPOS, Alzira, 1985: *Família portuguesa e família brasileira: paradigma europeu no mundo colonial*. Oporto: Centro de Estudos da Secretaria de Estado das Comunidades Portuguesas, 65 pp.

1191 CAMPOS, Alzira, 1986: 'Mulher e identidade social (o exemplo da emigrada portuguesa en São Paulo)', in *Migrare: Revista dos Seminários de Verão*. Lisbon: Secretaria de Estado das Comunidades Portuguesas, 77 pp.

1192   CAMPOS, Luis Edmundo de Arruda, 1987: *Alocação sócio-profissional e visão do mundo: portugueses proprietários de bares e padarias na região de Vila Mariana (São Paulo, Brasil)*. Oporto: Centro de Estudos da Secretaria de Estado das Comunidades Portugueses, 49 pp.

1193   CRUZ, Maria Antonieta, 1986-7: 'Agruras dos emigrantes portugueses no Brasil: contribução para o estudo do emigração portuguesa na segunda metade do século XIX', *RH/O*, no. 7, pp. 7-135.

1194   GOUVEIA, Horácio Bento de, 1948/9: 'Aspectos da emigração madeirense para o Brasil nos reinados de Dom João V e Dom José', in *Das artes e da história da Madeira*. Funchal.

1195   HAHNER, June E., 1976: 'Jacobinos versus Gallegos: urban radicals versus Portuguese immigrants in Rio de Janeiro in the 1890's', *JIASWA*, 18/2, pp. 125-54.

1196   KLEIN, Herbert S., 1991: 'The social and economic integration of Portuguese immigrants in Brazil in the late nineteenth and twentieth centuries', *JLAS*, 23/2, pp. 309-337.

1197   LEITE, Joaquim da Costa, 1987: 'Emigração portuguesa: a lei e os números (1855-1914)', *AS*, no. 97, pp. 463-480.

1198   MONTEIRO, Tânia Penido, 1985: *Portugueses na Bahia na segunda metade do século XIX. Emigração e comércio*. Oporto: Centro de Estudos da Secretaria de Estado das Comunidades Portuguesas, 189 pp.

1199   PAUL, Clotilde, 1986: *Associação Portuguesa da Baixada Santista*. Oporto: Centro de Estudos da Secretaria de Estado das Comunidades Portuguesas, 61 pp.

1200   PEDREIRA, Maria Emília, 1986: 'Valores tradicionais entre as mulheres portuguesas de Fortaleza', in *Primero encontro das portuguesas migrantes no associativismo e no jornalismo*. Oporto: Centro de Estudos da Secretaria de Estado das Comunidades Portuguesas, pp. 31-36.

1201   PEREIRA, Vanildo Rodrigues, 1985: *A convivência do Centro Português de Maringá com a comunidade do Norte do Paraná*. Oporto: Centro de Estudos da Secretaria de Estado das Comunidades Portuguesas, 79 pp.

1202   PESCATELLO, Ann Marie, 1970: *Both ends of the journey: an historical study of migration and change in Brazil and Portugal, 1889-1914*. PhD Thesis, University of California, Los Angeles.

1203   PORTELA, Irene, 1983: *Identidade étnica dos portugueses no Brasil: o caso das instituições luso-brasileiras*. Rio de Janeiro: Museu Nacional.

1204   PORTELA, Irene and Maria Ermelinda OLIVEIRA, 1987: *Migrantes portuguesas no Brasil: o paradoxo do retorno.* Lisbon: Centro de Estudos da Secretaria de Estado das Comunidades Portuguesas, 52 pp.

1205   ROCHA-TRINDADE, Maria Beatriz, 1987: 'Refluxos culturais da emigração portuguesa para o Brasil', in Gianfausto Rosoli, ed., *Emigrazione europee e popolo brasiliano.* Rome: Centro Studi Emigrazione, pp. 335-354.

1206   SANTOS, Mário Augusto da Silva, 1977: *O comércio português na Bahia, 1870-1930.* Centenário de Manoel Joaquim de Carvalho. Salvador: Irmão Paulo.

1207   SCHMITI, Lucy Maurício, 1985: *Comunidades portuguesas: fenómeno associativo no Estado do Paraná.* Oporto: Centro de Estudos da Secretaria de Estado das Comunidades Portuguesas, 71 pp.

1208   SERRÃO, Joel, 1976: 'A emigração portuguesa para o Brasil na segunda metade do século XIX (Esboço de problematização)', *JGSWGL*, vol. 13, pp. 84-106.

1209   SILVA, José-Gentil da, 1976: 'A emigração para América nos séculos 19 e 20 e a história nacional: os Portugueses e a América', *JGSWGL*, vol. 13, pp. 107-131.

1210   TORRES, José Pereira, 1987: *O homem Minhoto (das origens à diáspora). História da Casa do Minho do Rio de Janeiro.* Oporto: Centro de Estudos da Secretaria de Estado das Comunidades Portuguesas, 125 pp.

1211   VALLADARES, António Canavarra de, 1978: 'Os ascendentes ribeira-peneses do presidente brasileiro Afonso Pena', *RIHGB*, vol. 320.

Chile

See also: 128

Venezuela

1212   MADEIRA, 1971: *Os madeirenses na Venezuela* (conferência proferida na Casa da Madeira de Lisboa em 29 de Junho de 1971). Lisbon: Dongo-Ind. Gráfica Editora.

1213   SAIGNES, Miguel Acosta, 1977 (2nd ed.): *Historia de los portugueses en Venezuela.* Caracas: Librería Suma, 116 pp.

RUSSIAN

General

1214 KOMISSAROV, Boris Nikolaevic, 1983: 'Los primeros rusos en América Latina', *AL*, no. 10, pp. 41-56.

1215 KOROLEV, Nocolai, 1976: 'Emigración de Rusia a América Latina a fines del siglo XIX, comienzos del siglo XX', *JGSWGL*, vol. 13, pp. 31-37.

1216 STRELKO, Andrei, 1979: 'Análisis del problema de la emigración de Rusia a la América Latina (hasta el año 1917) en la URSS', in *La emigración europea a la América Latina: fuentes y estado de investigación (informes presentados a la IV Reunión de Historiadores Latinoamericanistas Europeos)*. Berlin: Colloquium Verlag (Bibliotheca Ibero-Americana), pp. 257-263.

See also: 341; 1419

Argentina

See: 341

Bolivia

See: 1074

Brazil

1217 COLFER, Michael A., 1985: *Morality, kindred, and ethnic boundary: a study of the Oregon Old Believers*. New York: AMS Press, 159 pp.

1218 UNITED NATIONS, 1967: 'The Old Believers: a story of faith and perseverance', *Monthly Newsletter (United Nations High Commissioner for Refugees)*, Geneva, no. 45, April.

Mexico

1219 BONIFAZ, M.E., 1983: 'La colonia rusa del valle de Guadalupe', *PA*, pp. 311-314.

1220   BOROVKOV, Antolii, 1988: 'Una colonia rusa en México', *AL*, no. 11, pp. 82-86.

1221   LIZIZIN, S., n.d.: *Secta religiosa molokane y la colonia rusa de Guadalupe*. Ensenada.

Paraguay

1222   BURR, Malcolm, 1935: 'Russians in Paraguay', *NCA*, 118/704, pp. 441-448.

1223   ECKSTEIN, Alejandro von, 1986: *Pitiantuta: la chispa que encendió la hoguera en el Chaco paraguayo*. Asunción: Dirección de Publicaciones, Fuerzas Armadas, 112 pp.

See also: 1437

Uruguay

1224   HOY ES HISTORIA, 1986: 'La Colonia San Javier: breve historia gráfica de su proceso fundacional', *HH*, 3/15, pp. 66-74.

SPANISH

Bibliography

1225   FISCHER DE FIGUEROA, Marie-Claire, 1987: 'La inmigración española en México: evaluación bibliográfica', in *Seminar on the Acquisition of Latin American Library Materials (SALALM)*. *Papers of the thirty-first annual meeting*. Madison: University of Wisconsin, pp. 163-187.

General

1226   DELGADO RIBAS, Josep M., 1989: 'La emigración española durante las décadas del comercio libre (1765-1820)', *SG*, 4/7, pp. 315-339.

1227   DIAZ, Janet W., 1983: 'Spanish Civil War and exile in the novels of Aub, Ayala and Sender', in Hans-Bernhard Moeller, ed., *Latin America and the literature of exile*. Heidelberg: Carl Winter Universitätsverlag, pp. 207-231.

1228   GALERSTEIN, Carolyn L., 1983: 'Outside-inside views of exile: Spanish women novelists and younger generation writers', in Hans-Bernhard Moeller, ed., *Latin America and the literature of exile*. Heidelberg: Carl Winter Universitätsverlag, pp 137-148.

1229   GRUGEL, Jean and Monica QUIJADA, 1990: 'Chile, Spain and Latin America: the right of asylum at the onset of the Second World War', *JLAS*, 22/2, pp. 353-374.

1230   HERNÁNDEZ GARCÍA, Julio, 1979: 'Informe sobre fuentes existentes en España para un estudio de la emigración a Iberoamérica durante el siglo XIX', in *La emigración europea a la América Latina: fuentes y estado de investigación (informes presentados a la IV Reunión de Historiadores Latinoamericanistas Europeos)*. Berlin: Colloquium Verlag (Bibliotheca Ibero-Americana), pp. 9-52.

1231   PIKE, Frederick B., 1971: 'Hispanismo and the non-revolutionary Spanish immigrant in Spanish America, 1900-1930', *IAEA*, 25/2, pp. 3-30.

1232   RAMOS PÉREZ, Demetrio, 1976: 'Fases de la emigración española a Hispanoamérica en el siglo XIX', *JGSWGL*, vol. 13, pp. 151-173.

1233   SÁNCHEZ-ALBORNOZ, Nicolás, 1988: 'Medio siglo de emigración masiva de España hacia América', in Nicolás Sánchez-Albornoz, ed., *Españoles hacia América: la emigración en masa, 1880-1930*. Madrid:

Alianza Editorial, pp. 13-32.

1234   SÁNCHEZ-ALBORNOZ, Nicolás, 1990: 'Las etapas de la migración española a América Latina', *AR*, no. 536-537, tomo 136-137, pp. 15-24.

1235   SÁNCHEZ ALONSO, Blanca, 1989: 'La visión contemporánea de la emigración española', *EML*, no. 13, pp. 439-466.

See also: 450; 461

Argentina

1236   ARMUS, Diego, 1984: 'Notas sobre el impacto inmigratorio ultramarino a la Argentina y la visión de los protagonistas', *RI*, 44/174, pp. 491-505.

1237   CIGNETTI, Ana María, 1989: *La inmigración española en la Patagonia.* México, DF: Instituto Panamericano de Geografía e Historia, 112 pp.

1238   CORTÉS CONDE, Roberto, 1988: 'Migración, cambio agrícola y políticas de protección. El caso argentino', in Nicolás Sánchez-Albornoz, ed., *Españoles hacia América: la emigración en masa, 1880-1930.* Madrid: Alianza Editorial, pp. 235-248.

1239   DÍAZ MELIÁN, Mafalda Victoria, 1980: 'Emigración española hacia la Argentina en la década del 80', *BIHAA*, 16/26, pp. 117-161.

1240   FERNÁNDEZ, Alejandro E., 1984: 'Una comunidad española en Santa Fe y su Sociedad de Socorros Mutuos', *SE*, 21/74, pp. 186-207.

1241   FERNÁNDEZ, Alejandro E., 1990: 'La colectividad española de Buenos Aires y el asociacionismo étnico', *AR*, no. 536-537, tomo 136-137, pp. 25-51.

1242   FERNÁNDEZ, Alejandro E., 1987: 'El mutualismo español en Buenos Aires, 1890-1920'. Un estudio de caso', *CHR*, no. 8.

1243   FERNÁNDEZ, Alejandro E., 1987: 'Patria y cultura. Aspectos de la acción de la élite española de Buenos Aires (1890-1920)', *EML*, no. 6-7, pp. 291-308.

1244   FERNÁNDEZ, Alejandro E., 1989: 'El mutualismo español en un barrio de Buenos Aires: San José de Flores, (1890-1900)', *EML*, no. 13, pp. 609-642.

1245   GALLIARI, Mabel and Ofelia PIANETTO, 1989: 'La inserción social de los inmigrantes españoles en la ciudad de Córdoba 1870-1914', *EML*, no.

13, pp. 583-608.

1246   GALIMARINI, Hugo Raúl, 1986: 'Los españoles de Buenos Aires después de la Revolución de Mayo: la suerte de una minoría desposeída del poder', *RI*, 46/178, pp. 561-592.

1247   MARQUIEGUI, Dedier Norberto, 1989: 'La inmigración española en Luján (1880-1920)', *EML*, no. 13, pp. 525-562.

1248   MARSAL, Juan F., 1969: *Hacer la América: autobiografía de un inmigrante español en la Argentina*. Buenos Aires: Editorial del Instituto Torcuato di Tella, 434 pp.

1249   MOYA, José Carlos, 1986: 'Notas sobre las fuentes para el estudio de la inmigración española en Buenos Aires', *EML*, no. 4, pp. 497-504.

1250   MOYA, José Carlos, 1980: *Spaniards in Buenos Aires: patterns of immigration and adaptation, 1852-1930*. PhD Thesis, Rutgers University.

1251   MOYA, José Carlos, 1980, 1989: 'Parientes y extraños: actitudes hacia los inmigrantes españoles en la Argentina en el siglo XIX y comienzos del siglo XX', *EML*, no. 13, pp. 499-524.

1252   NASCIMBENE, Mario C.G., 1985: 'Evolución de la población española e italiana en la Argentina (1869-1970): un enfoque comparado', in *La inmigración a América Latina (primeras jornadas internacionales sobre la migración en América)*. México, DF: Instituto Panamericano de Geografía e Historia (Serie inmigración, tomo 2), pp. 113-134.

1253   ORSATTI, Alvaro, 1982: *Españoles en Argentina: características personales y económicas*. Buenos Aires: Centro Interamericano para el Desarrollo Social (Serie Informes Parciales – Migraciones Laborales en Argentina, no. 7), 23 pp.

1254   QUIJADA MAURIÑO, Mónica, 1989: 'Política inmigratoria del primer peronismo: las negociaciones con España', *REELC*, no. 47, pp. 43-64.

1255   ROCAMORA, Juan, 1989: 'El exilio médico en la Argentina', *CH*, no. 473-474, pp. 63-74.

1256   SÁNCHEZ ALONSO, Blanca, 1988: 'La emigración española a la Argentina, 1880-1930,' in Nicolás Sánchez-Albornoz, ed., *Españoles hacia América: la emigración en masa, 1880-1930*. Madrid: Alianza Editorial, pp. 205-234.

1257   SCHWARZSTEIN, Dora, 1988: 'Historia oral y memoria del exilio: reflexiones sobre los republicanos españoles en la Argentina', *AEH*, segunda época, no. 13, pp. 235-256.

1258   VIDAURRETA DE TJARKS, Alicia, 1982: 'Spanish immigration to Argentina, 1870-1930', *JGSWGL*, vol. 19, pp. 285-319.

1259   YÁÑEZ GALLARDO, César, 1989: 'Argentina como país de destino. La emigración española entre 1860-1930', *EML*, no. 13, pp. 467-498.

1260   ZAGO, Manrique, ed., 1985: *Los españoles de la Argentina*. Buenos Aires: Manrigue Zago Ediciones.

See also: 1426

Brazil

1261   GONZÁLEZ MARTÍNEZ, Elda Evangelina, 1990: 'Los pequeños propietarios en los Núcleos Coloniales del Estado de São Paulo. Un intento frustrado de participación española', *AR*, no. 536-537, tomo 136-137, pp. 127-142.

1262   JORDÃO, Antônio, 1964: 'O imigrante espanhol em São Paulo: principais conclusões de uma pesquisa', *SA*, 26/2, pp. 249-252.

1263   KLEIN, Herbert S., 1989: 'La integración social y económica de los inmigrantes españolas en Brasil', *RHE*, 7/2, pp. 439-460.

1264   SOUZA-MARTINS, José de, 1988: 'La inmigración española en Brasil y la formación de la fuerza de trabajo en la economía cafetalera, 1880-1930', in Nicolás Sánchez-Albornoz, ed., *Españoles hacia América: la emigración en masa, 1880-1930*. Madrid: Alianza Editorial, pp. 249-269.

Chile

See: 128

Cuba

1265   BERGAD, Laird W., 1985: 'Spanish migration to Cuba in the nineteenth century', *AC*, 4-5, pp. 174-204.

1266   GONZÁLEZ SUÁREZ, Dominga, 1988: 'La inmigración española en Cuba', *ED/Hav*, no. 102, pp. 92-107.

1267   IGLESIAS GARCÍA, Fe, 1988: 'Características de la inmigración española en Cuba (1904-1930)', *ED/Hav*, no. 103, pp. 76-101.

1268   IGLESIAS GARCÍA, Fe, 1988: 'Características de la inmigración española en Cuba, 1904-1930', in Nicolás Sánchez-Albornoz, ed., *Españoles hacia América: la emigración en masa, 1880-1930*. Madrid: Alianza Editorial, pp. 270-295.

1269   KENNY, Michael, 1961: 'Twentieth century Spanish expatriates in Cuba: a sub-culture?', *AQ*, 34/2, pp. 85-93.

1270   NARANJO OROVIO, V., Consuelo, 1984: 'Análisis histórico de la emigración española a Cuba, 1900-1959', *RI*, 44/174, pp. 507-527.

1271   NARANJO OROVIO, V., Consuelo, 1987: *Cuba vista por el emigrante español a la isla, 1900-1959: un ensayo de historia oral*. Madrid: Centro de Estudios Históricos, Departamento de Historia de América, 164 pp.

1272   NARANJO OROVIO, Consuelo and Alfredo MORENO CEBRIAN, 1990: 'La repatriación forzosa y las crisis económicas cubanas: 1921-1933', *AR*, no. 536-537, tomo 136-137, pp. 203-230.

Dominican Republic

1273   MALAGÓN, Javier, 1981: 'Los profesores españoles exiliados en la Universidad de Santo Domingo (1939-1949)', *AR*, 108/423, pp. 49-63.

1274   NARANJO OROVIO, V. Consuelo, 1987: 'Transterrados españoles en las Antillas: un acercamiento a su vida cotidiana', *AEA*, vol. 44, pp. 521-548.

1275   VEGA, Bernardo, 1984: *La migración española de 1939 y los inicios del marxismo-leninismo en la República Dominicana*. Santo Domingo: Fundación Cultural Dominicana, 208 pp.

See also: 139

Mexico

1276   ARTÍS E., Gloria, 1979: 'La organización social y socialización de los españoles en las ciudades de México y Tehuacán', in *Inmigrantes y refugiados españoles en México (siglo XX)*. México, DF: Ediciones de La Casa Chata, pp. 293-336.

1277   CARREÑO, Alberto María, 1942: *Los españoles en el México independiente (un siglo de beneficencia)*. México, DF: Impr. M.L. Sanchez, 476 pp.

1278   DOMÍNGUEZ PRATS, Pilar, 1990: 'Las exiliadas españolas en México (1939-1950)', *AR*, no. 536-537, tomo 136-137, pp. 231-247.

1279   FAGEN, Patricia W., 1973: *Exiles and citizens: Spanish Republicans in Mexico*. Austin: University of Texas Press, 250 pp.

1280   FISCHER DE FIGUEROA, Marie Claire, 1986: 'La inmigración intelectual española en México. Evaluación bibliográfica', *FI*, 27/1, pp. 132-153.

1281   GARCÍA ACOSTA, Virginia, 1979: 'La integración económica de los españoles en la ciudad de Puebla y los asturianos en el Distrito Federal', in *Inmigrantes y refugiados españoles en México (siglo XX)*. México, DF: Ediciones de La Casa Chata, pp. 93-164.

1282   GONZÁLEZ LOSCERTALES, Vicente, 1977: 'Política del Porfiriato, emigración peninsular y emigración canaria a México: análisis comparativo de la emigración peninsular y canaria (1882-1911)', in *I coloquio de historia Canario-Americano (Las Palmas, 1976)*, pp. 384-403.

1283   GONZÁLEZ LOSCERTALES, Vicente, 1979: 'Bases para el análisis socioeconómico de la colonia española de México en 1910', *RI*, 39/155-158, pp. 267-295.

1284   GONZÁLEZ LOSCERTALES, Vicente, 1983: 'El empresariado español en Puebla (1880-1916). Surgimiento y crisis de un grupo de poder', in *Capitales, empresarios y obreros europeos en América Latina (Actas del 6° Congreso de AHILA, Stockholm, 25-28 de Mayo 1981)*. Stockholm: Instituto de Estudios Latinoamericanos (monografías, no. 8, tomo 2), pp. 468-492.

1285   GUARNER, Vicente, 1988: 'La inmigración de médicos españoles de 1939 y la medicina en México', *CA*, no. 7, nueva época, pp. 16-28.

1286   ICAZURIAGA, Carmen, 1979: 'Españoles de Veracruz y vascos del Distrito Federal: su ubicación en la estructura económica de México', in *Inmigrantes y refugiados españoles en México (siglo XX)*. México, DF: Ediciones de La Casa Chata, pp. 165-224.

1287   KENNY, Michael, 1979: 'Emigración, inmigración, remigración: el ciclo migratorio de los españoles en México', in *Inmigrantes y refugiados españoles en México (siglo XX)*. México, DF: Ediciones de La Casa Chata, pp. 15-90.

1288   LEÓN-PORTILLA, Ascensión H. de, 1978: *España desde México: vida y testimonio de transterrados*. México, DF: Universidad Nacional Autónoma de México, 465 pp.

1289   LIDA, Clara E., 1985: 'Inmigrantes españoles durante el porfiriato', *HM*, 35/2, pp. 219-239.

1290   LIDA, Clara E., 1988: 'Los españoles en México. Del Porfiriato a la Post-Revolución', in Nicolás Sánchez-Albornoz, ed., *Españoles hacia América: la emigración en masa, 1880-1930*. Madrid: Alianza Editorial, pp. 322-342.

1291   MALAGÓN BARCELÓ, Javier, 1980: 'El exiliado político español en México (1939-1977)', *AR*, 105/409, pp. 25-36.

1292   SIMS, Harold, 1975: *La expulsión de los españoles de México, 1821-1828*. México, DF: Sección de Obras de Historia, Fondo de Cultura Económica, 300 pp.

1293   SIMS, Harold, 1981: 'Los exiliados españoles de México en 1829', *HM*, 30/3, pp. 391-414.

1294   SIMS, Harold, 1990: *The expulsion of Mexico's Spaniards, 1821-1836*. Pittsburgh: University of Pittsburgh Press, 277 pp.

1295   STEWARD, Luther, Jr., 1965: 'Spanish journalism in Mexico, 1867-1879', *HAHR*, 45/3, pp. 422-433.

1296   SUÁREZ, Clara Elena, 1979: 'Organización social y socialización de los españoles en las ciudades de México y Tehuacán', in *Inmigrantes y refugiados españoles en México (siglo XX)*. México, DF: Ediciones de La Casa Chata, pp. 225-293.

1297   TORRE BLANCO, José, 1976: *Uno de tantos: un médico republicano español refugiado en México*. México, DF: Colección Málaga, 386 pp.

1298   XIRAU, Ramón, 1988: 'España vista desde el exilio en México durante más de 25 años', *CV*, no. 50, pp. 81-88.

Paraguay

1299   PLÁ, Josephina, 1985: *Españoles en la cultura del Paraguay*. Asunción: Ed. Araverá, 427 pp.

Puerto Rico

1300   CIFRE DE LOUBRIEL, Estella, 1975: *La formación del pueblo puertorriqueño: la contribución de los catalanes, baleáricos y valencianos*. San Juan: Instituto de Cultura Puertorriqueña, 485 pp.

1301   CIFRE DE LOUBRIEL, Estella, 1989: *La formación del pueblo puertorri-queño: la contribución de los gallegos, asturianos y santanderinos*. Río Piedras: Editorial de la Universidad de Puerto Rico, 585 pp.

1302   SANTIAGO-MARAZZI, Rosa, 1974: 'El impacto de la inmigración a Puerto Rico, 1800-1830: análisis estadístico', *RCS*, 18, pp. 1-42.

1303   SANTIAGO-MARAZZI, Rosa, 1986-7: 'La inmigración de mujeres españoles a Puerto Rico en el período colonial español', *HO*, Feb./Dec., pp. 154-165.

1304   SONESSON, Birgit, 1988: 'La emigración española a Puerto Rico. ¿Continuidad o irrupción bajo nueva soberanía?' in Nicolás Sánchez-Albornoz, ed., *Españoles hacia América: la emigración en masa, 1880-1930*. Madrid: Alianza Editorial, pp. 296-321.

Uruguay

1305   AINSA, Fernando, 1989: 'El exilio español en Uruguay', *CH*, no. 473-474, pp. 159-170.

1306   NAVARRO-AZCUE, Concepción, 1990: 'La emigración española a Uruguay: 1930-1935', *AR*, no. 536-537, tomo 136-137, pp. 99-125.

1307   RIAL ROADE, Juan, 1985: *Inmigración y urbanización en el Río de la Plata: con especial referencia a la corriente española y al caso de Montevideo, Uruguay*. Montevideo: Centro de Informaciones y Estudios del Uruguay, 73 pp.

Venezuela

1308   HERNÁNDEZ ARVELO, Miguel Ángel, 1990: 'El proceso de la inmigración española en Venezuela (1939-1980), *BANH/Car*, 73/290, pp. 97-108.

1309   HERNÁNDEZ ARVELO, Miguel A., 1990: 'El proceso de la inmigración española en Venezuela: 1939-1970', *AR*, no. 536-537, tomo 136-137, pp. 177-188.

Andalucian

General

1310   BERNAL, Antonio M., 1988: 'La emigración de Andalucía', in Nicolás

Sánchez-Albornoz, ed., *Españoles hacia América: la emigración en masa, 1880-1930*. Madrid: Alianza Editorial, pp. 143-165.

Argentina

1311   FERRÁ DE BARTOL, Margarita, 1987: 'La comunidad andaluza en San Juan, República Argentina', in *Andalucía y América en el siglo XX*. Seville: Escuela de Estudios Hispano-Americanos, pp. 197-244.

1312   SCHWARZSTEIN, Dora, 1987: 'El exilio andaluz en la Argentina', in *Andalucía y América en el siglo XX*. Seville: Escuela de Estudios Hispano-Americanos, pp. 173-196.

Brazil

1313   GONZÁLEZ MARTÍNEZ, Elda E. and Consuelo NARANJO OROVIO, 1987: 'Aproximaciones cuantitativas y aspectos cualitativos de la emigración andaluza a Brasil y Cuba (1880-1940)', in *Andalucía y América en el siglo XX*. Seville: Escuela de Estudios Hispano-Americanos, pp. 245-274.

Cuba

See: 1313

Asturian

General

1314   ANES, Rafael, 1988: 'La gran emigración asturiana', in Nicolás Sánchez Albornoz, ed., *Españoles hacia América: la emigración en masa, 1880-1930*. Madrid: Alianza Editorial, pp. 33-52.

1315   GARCIÁ LÓPEZ, Héctor Ramón, 1989: 'Consecuencias económicas de la emigración asturiana a América: las remesas', *EML*, no. 13, pp. 643-659.

1316   OJEDA, Germán and José Luis SAN MIGUEL, 1985: *Campesinos, emigrantes, indianos: emigración y economía en Asturias, 1830-1930*. Salinas (Asturias): Ayalga Ediciones, 157 pp.

1317   LLORDÉN, Moisés, 1988: 'Los inicios de la emigración asturiana a América. 1858-1870', in Nicolás Sánchez-Albornoz, ed., *Españoles hacia América: la emigración en masa, 1880-1930*. Madrid: Alianza Editorial, pp. 53-65.

1318   MARTÍNEZ CACHERO, Luis Alfonso, 1976: *La emigración asturiana a América*. Salinas (Asturias): Ayalga Ediciones, 156 pp.

1319   MARTÍNEZ FERNÁNDEZ, Jesús, 1984: 'Intelectuales del occidente asturiano en la emigración a las Américas', *BIEA*, 38/113, pp. 957-978.

1320   SARO MORALES, María Cruz 1988: 'Las fundaciones de los Indianos en Asturias', in Nicolás Sánchez-Albornoz, ed., *Españoles hacia América: la emigración en masa, 1880-1930*. Madrid: Alianza Editorial, pp. 66-79.

See also: 1362

Chile

1321   MARTINIC, Mateo, 1988: 'La emigración asturiana en Magallanes', *BIEA*.

Mexico

See: 1281

Puerto Rico

See: 1301

Basque

General

1322   DOUGLASS, William A. and Jon BILBAO, 1975: *Amerikanuak: Basques in the New World*. Reno: University of Nevada Press, 519 pp.

1323   FERNÁNDEZ DE PINEDO, Emiliano, 1988: 'Los movimientos migratorios vascos, en especial hacia América', in Nicolás Sánchez-Albornoz, ed., *Españoles hacia América: la emigración en masa, 1880-1930*. Madrid: Alianza Editorial, pp. 105-122.

Argentina

1324   GOYECHEA, Juan, 1975: *Los gauchos vascos*. Buenos Aires: Edit. Vasca Ekin.

1325   PILDAIN SALAZAR, Pilar, 1984: *Ir a América: la emigración vasca a América (Guipúzcoa 1840-1870)*. San Sebastián: Grupo Doctor Camino, 245 pp.

1326   SOULES, María Inés, 1976: 'El aporte vasco a dos ciudades americanas: Boise (EE.UU.) y Olavarría (Argentina)', in *Asociación argentina de estudios americanos, X Jornadas (Buenos Aires)*, pp. 224-237.

Chile

1327   SANTOS MARTÍNEZ, Pedro, 1987: 'La inmigración en Chile: el caso de los colonos vascos (1882-1883)', *HI*, 22, pp. 287-311.

Colombia

See: 990

Mexico

1328   GONZÁLEZ CALZADA, Manuel, 1975: *México vasco*. México, DF: B. Costa-Amic Editor, 229 pp.

1329   LEGARRETA, Dorothy, 1984: *The Guernica generation: Basque refugee children of the Spanish Civil War*. Reno: University of Nevada Press, 396 pp.

1330   PAYÁ VALERA, Emeterio, 1985: *Los niños españoles de Morelia. (El exilio infantil en México)*. México, DF: Edamex, 256 pp.

Peru

See: 161

Puerto Rico

See: 1301

Uruguay

1331   ARBIZA, Orlando, M., 1987: *El aporte vasco al Departamento de Artigas*. Montevideo: Ediciones de la Plaza, 257 pp.

1332   OTAEGUI, Tomás, 1943: *Los vascos en el Uruguay*. Buenos Aires: Edit. Vasca Ekin.

See also: 1325

Venezuela

1333   PASTOR CASTILLO, Roberto, 1979: *Euskalherria en Venezuela.* San Sebastián: Ed. Vascas, 366 pp.

Canary Islander

General

1334   ALBELO MARTÍN, María Cristina, 1982: 'Canarias y los indianos repatriados durante la primera mitad del s. XIX', in *IV Coloquio de Historia Canario-Americana* (Las Palmas), tomo 2, pp. 513-536.

1335   ALBELO MARTÍN, María Cristina, 1985: 'Trabajadores canarios en América: algunos ejemplos de contratos', in *V Coloquio de Historia Canario-Americana* (Las Palmas, 1982), tomo 1, pp. 341-406.

1336   ARMAS, Marcelo, 1984: 'Canarias en América: el otro archipiélago en 1992', in *VI Jornadas de estudios Canarias-América*, pp. 151-164.

1337   CALLE MURGUÍA, Angel Luis de la, 1984: 'Canarios en América: una presencia integradera', in *VI Jornadas de estudios Canarias-América*, pp. 103-114.

1338   GUERRO BALFAGÓN, Enrique, 1960: 'La emigración de los naturales de las Islas Canarias a las Repúblicas del Río de La Plata en la primera mitad del siglo XIX', *AEAT*, no. 6, pp. 493-517.

1339   HERNÁNDEZ GARCÍA, Julio, 1976: 'Algunos aspectos de la emigración de las Islas Canarias a Hispanoamérica en la segunda mitad del siglo XIX (1840-1895)', *JGSWGL*, vol. 13, pp. 132-150.

1340   HERNÁNDEZ GARCÍA, Julio, 1977: 'La travesía de los emigrantes canarios a América durante el siglo XIX y principios del XX: una forma de esclavitud', in *I Coloquio de historia canario-americana* (Las Palmas, 1976), pp. 356-381.

1341   MACÍAS, Antonio M., 1988: 'Un siglo de emigración canaria, 1830-1930', in Nicolás Sánchez-Albornoz, ed., *Españoles hacia América: la emigración en masa, 1880-1930*. Madrid: Alianza Editorial, pp. 166-202.

Argentina

1342   ENSINCK, Oscar Luis, 1985: 'Inmigrantes canarios en Rosario (Argentina)', in *V Coloquio de historia canario-americana* (Las Palmas, 1982), tomo 1, pp. 219-247.

1343   MARCO, Miguel Angel de, 1985: 'Las expediciones de emigrados canarios a Buenos Aires de 1833 y 1836', in *V Coloquio de historia canario-americana* (Las Palmas, 1982), tomo 1, pp. 315-339.

See also: 1338

Brazil

1344   SALOMÃO, Lilian Fonseca, 1985: 'Canariens au Brésil au début du XIX siècle: une immigration utile pour un pays neuf', in *V Coloquio de historia canario-americana* (Las Palmas, 1982), tomo 1, pp. 453-462.

Costa Rica

1345   CUESTA DOMINGO, Mariano, 1985: 'La presencia de España en Costa Rica. Aporte canario: notas para su estudio', in *V Coloquio de historia canario-americana* (Las Palmas, 1982), tomo 1, pp. 537-571.

Cuba

1346   HERNÁNDEZ GARCÍA, Julio, 1979: 'La planificación de la emigración canaria a Cuba y Puerto Rico', in *II Coloquio de historia canario-americana* (Las Palmas, 1977) pp. 199-238.

1347   LORENZO PERERA, Manuel J., 1985: 'Consideraciones sobre la emigración a Cuba. Isla de El Herro, Canarios', in *V Coloquio de historia canario-americana* (Las Palmas, 1982), tomo 1, pp. 407-453.

1348   NARANJO OROVIO, Consuelo, 1986: 'Canarios en Cuba, s. XX', in *VII coloquio de historia canario-americana* (Las Palmas).

Mexico

See: 1346

Puerto Rico

1349   ÁLVAREZ NAZARIO, Manuel, 1966: 'La inmigración canaria en Puerto Rico durante los siglos XVIII y XIX', *RICP*, vol. 9, pp. 52-56.

Uruguay

1350   FERNÁNDEZ, David W., 1963/4: 'Los canarios en el Uruguay', *RHC*, nos. 141-148, pp. 56-69.

1351   MARTÍNEZ DÍAZ, Nelson, 1978: 'La inmigración canaria en Uruguay durante la primera mitad del siglo XIX: una sociedad para el transporte de colonos', *RI*, 38/151-2, pp. 349-402.

1352   MARTÍNEZ DÍAZ, Nelson, 1985: 'La emigración clandestina desde las Islas Canarias al Uruguay. Formas de incorporación social', in *V coloquio de historia canario-americana* (Las Palmas, 1982), tomo 1, pp. 85.

1353   MARTÍNEZ DÍAZ, N., 1990: 'La emigración canaria al Uruguay: 1830-1860', *AR*, no. 536-537, tomo 136-137, pp. 53-73.

1354   MUSSO AMBROSI, Luis Alberto, 1988: 'Españoles canarios en el Uruguay (años 1830-1850)', *EHSEA*, no. 3-4, pp. 155-163.

See also: 1338

Venezuela

1355   BLANCO MONTESDEOCA, Joaquín, 1977: 'Emigración frustrada: Las Palmas-Venezuela (1948-1950)', in *I Coloquio de historia canario-americana* (Las Palmas, 1976), pp. 406-415.

1356   HERNÁNDEZ GARCÍA, Julio, 1982: *Los canarios en la gestación de la República de Venezuela, 1831-1863*. Santa Cruz de Tenerife: Ed. Centro de la Cultura Popular Canaria.

1357   HERNÁNDEZ GARCÍA, Julio and Manuel HERNÁNDEZ GONZÁLEZ, 1990: 'La emigración canaria a Venezuela en el siglo XIX', *AR*, no. 536-537, pp. 161-175.

Catalan

General

1358   YÁÑEZ GALLARDO, César, 1988: 'Cataluña: un caso de emigración temprana', in Nicolás Sánchez-Albornoz, ed., *Españoles hacia América: la emigración en masa, 1880-1930*. Madrid: Alianza Editorial, pp. 123-142.

Argentina

1359   DELGADO RIBAS, Josep M., 1983: 'La emigración española a Argentina durante la época del comercio libre, 1765-1820: "el ejemplo catalán"', *BA*, no. 32.

Cuba

1360   ROY, Joaquin, 1988: *Catalunya a Cuba*. Barcelona: Editorial Barcino, 193 pp.

Puerto Rico

See: 1300

Uruguay

1361   PARIS DE ODDONE, María Blanca, 1960: *Figuras e instituciones catalanas en el Uruguay*. Montevideo: Edit. Florensa y Lafón.

Galician

General

1362   NARANJO, Consuelo and GONZÁLEZ, Evangelina, 1987: 'Emigración gallega y asturiana en el s. XX a la Argentina, Brasil, Uruguay y Cuba', *IA*, May-June.

1363   VÁZQUEZ, Alejandro, 1988: 'La emigración gallega: migrantes, transporte y remesas', in Nicolás Sánchez-Albornoz, ed., *Españoles hacia América: la emigración en masa, 1880-1930*. Madrid: Alianza Editorial, pp. 80-104.

Argentina

1364   NUÑEZ SEIXAS, Xosé Manoel, 1990: 'Emigración y nacionalismo gallego en Argentina 1879-1936', *EML*, no. 15-16, pp. 379-406.

1365   PALMÁS, Ricardo, 1978: *A emigración galega na Arxentina*. La Coruña: Ediciós de Castro, 49 pp.

1366   PÉREZ-PRADO, Antonio, 1973: *Los Gallegos y Buenos Aires*. Buenos Aires: La Bastilla.

1367   PÉREZ-PRADO, Antonio, 1973: *Los Gallegos en la Argentina*. Buenos Aires: Ed. La Bastilla.

Brazil

1368   DOS SANTOS, Ricardo Evaristo, 1987: 'Pintura gallega en Brasil (1890-1935)', *BABA*, no. 65, pp. 246-250.

1369   DOS SANTOS, Ricardo Evaristo, 1987: 'Vida intelectual gallega en América: aporte Brasil (Estado de São Paulo, 1890-1950)', in *Actas: I^{as} jornadas presencia de España en América: aportación gallega* (Pazo de Mariñán), pp. 383-388.

Cuba

1370   LECUYER, Marie-Claude, 1987: *Immigration blanche à Cuba: L'expérience galicienne (1853-1855)*. Toulouse: Université de Toulouse-Le Mirail.

1371   NARANJO OROVIO, Consuelo, 1988: *Del campo a la bodega: recuerdos de gallegos en Cuba (siglo XX)*. La Coruña: Edición do Castro, 269 pp.

1372   NEIRA VILAS, Xosé, 1983: *Gallegos en el Golfo de México*. Havana: Ed. Letras Cubanas, 197 pp.

1373   NEIRA VILAS, Xosé, 1985: *A prensa galega de Cuba*. La Coruña: Ed. do Castro, 169 pp.

Puerto Rico

See: 1301

Uruguay

1374   GAGIAO VILA, Pilar, 1990: 'Aporte cultural de la inmigración gallega en Montevideo: 1879-1930', *AR*, no. 536-537, tomo 136-137, pp. 75-97.

1375   GAJIAO [GAGIAO] VILA, Pilar, 1986: 'Los gallegos en el Uruguay contemporáneo y a través de la historia', *HH*, 3/18, pp. 26-37.

1376   GAGIAO VILA, Pilar, 1989: 'Problemas planteados en el estudio de la inmigración gallega en Montevideo, (1900-1970)', *EML*, no. 13, pp. 563-582.

1377   ZUBILLAGA, Carlos, 1966: *Los gallegos en el Uruguay: apuntes para una historia de la inmigración gallega hasta fines del siglo XIX*. Montevideo: Ediciones del Banco de Galicia, 233 pp.

1378   ZUBILLAGA, Carlos, 1988: 'La inmigración gallega y los orígenes del sindicalismo uruguayo', *EML*, no. 9, pp. 179-198.

Venezuela

See: 1308; 1309

Valencian

Argentina

1379   MAIDA, Esther Lidia, 1971: *La colonización de Vicente Blasco Ibáñez y el contingente valenciano en el Alto Valle del Río Negro; formación de la colonia Cervantes*. Viedma: Centro Provincial de Documentación e Información Educativa y Social.

Puerto Rico

See: 1300

SWEDISH

General

1380   ÅBERG, Alf, 1984: *De första utvandrarna: svenska öden i Nord-och Sylamerika under 1800-talets första hälft*. Stockholm: Natur och Kultur, 310 pp.

1381   FLODELL, Sven Arne, 1974: *Tierra Nueva. Svensk grupputvandring till Latinamerika. Integration och församlingsbildning*. Uppsala: Studia Missionalia Upsaliensia, 217 pp.

1382   MÖRNER, Magnus, 1980: 'La imagen de América Latina en Suecia en los siglos XIX y XX', *EL*, no. 6, pt. 1, pp. 237-285.

1383   ROGBERG, Martin, 1954: *Svenskar i Latinamerika: pionjäröden och nutida insatser*. Lindqvists förlag, 135 pp.

1384   RUNBLOM, Harald, 1976: 'Swedish emigration to Latin America', in Harald Runblom and Hans Norman, eds., *From Sweden to America*. Minneapolis: University of Minnesota Press and Uppsala: Acta Universitatis Upsaliensis, pp. 301-310.

1385   RUNBLOM, Harald, 1979: 'La emigración sueca', in *La emigración europea a la América Latina: fuentes y estado de investigación (informes presentados a la IV Reunión de Historiadores Latinoamericanistas Europeos)*. Berlin: Colloquium Verlag (Bibliotheca Ibero-Americana), pp. 113-136.

1386   RUNBLOM, Harald, 1987: 'Nordic immigrants in Latin America', in Hans Norman and Harald Runblum, eds., *Transatlantic connections: Nordic migration to the New World after 1800*. Oslo: Norwegian University Press, pp. 175-182.

1387   STANG, Gudmund, 1976: 'La emigración escandinava a la América Latina, 1800-1940', *JGSWGL*, vol. 13, pp. 293-330.

Argentina

1388   FLODELL, Gunvor, 1986: *Misiones-Svenska: Språkbevarande och språkpåverkan i en sydamerikansk talgemenskap*. Uppsala: Institutionen för Nordiska Språk, 189 pp.

1389   PEHRSON, Gerda, 1965: *Floden tog.* Stockholm: LTs förlag, 175 pp.

1390   PEHRSON, Gerda, 1970: *Svenska pionjärer i Sydamerika.* Stockholm: LTs förlag, 126 pp.

1391   PEHRSON, Gerda, 1978: *Dona Ida och andra emigrantöden.* Laholm: Settern, 110 pp.

1392   WICKSTRÖM, Lloyd Jorge, 1989: *Del Yerbal Viejo a Obera: los suecos en Misiones.* Posadas, 239 pp.

See also: 361

Brazil

1393   FRIBORG, Göran, 1988: *Brasiliensvenskarna: utvandring, invandring, bosättning 1850-1940.* Växjö: Emigrantinstitutets (Skriftserie, Nr 5), 132 pp.

1394   KLASSON, Maj and Elisabeth OLANDER, 1987: *Till Brasilien 1891: om emigranter och återvändare.* Linköping: Kulturbyggares förlag, 194 pp.

See also: 1389

Colombia

1395   JARAMILLOS, Gabriel Giraldo, 1960: *Colombia y Suecia: relaciones culturales.* Madrid: "Insula", 170 pp.

Costa Rica

1396   BERGGREN, Karl, 1983: *Svenska Kolonien "Nueva Suecia", San Carlos, Costa Rica.* Uppsala: Harold Wretman, 32 pp.

See also: 133

Cuba

1397   NYSTRÖM, John A., 1988: 'La colonia sueca de Bayate', *DC*, no. 11.

1398   SARUSKY, Jaime, 1986: *Los fantasmas de Omaja.* Santiago de Cuba: Unión de Escritores y Artistas de Cuba, 117 pp.

SWISS

Bibliography

1399   NICOULIN, Martin and Béatrice ZIEGLER, 1975: *Emigration suisse en Amérique latine (1815-1939): essai bibliographique*. Bern: Bibliographique Nationale Suisse, 69 pp.

General

1400   ARLETTAZ, Gerald, 1979: *Emigration et colonisation suisse en Amérique 1815-1918*. Bern: Archives Fédérales Suisses (Etudes et sources, no. 5), 237 pp.

1401   ARLETTAZ, Gérald, Martin NICOULIN, Hans Werner TOBLER, Berthold WESSENDORF and Béatrice ZIEGLER, 1979: 'Emigración europea a América Latina: Suiza', in *La emigración europea a la América Latina: fuentes y estado de investigación (informes presentados a la IV Reunión de Historiadores Latinoamericanistas Europeos)*. Berlin: Colloquium Verlag (Bibliotheca Ibero-Americana), pp. 195-210.

1402   PEDRAZZINI, Augusto O., 1962: *L'emigrazione ticinese nell'America del Sud (2 vols.)*. Locarno: Tipi Grafica Pedrazzini, vol. 1: 440 pp.; vol. 2: 311 pp.

Argentina

1403   BLACHE, Martha, 1985: 'El folklore del inmigrante en Esperanza, Argentina. Elementos de cohesión y de fricción en el proceso colonizador de Esperanza', *FA*, no. 41-42, pp. 111-125.

1404   CARRON, Alexandre and Christophe CARRON, 1986: *Nos cousins d'Amérique: histoire de l'émigration valaisanne au XIXe. siècle*. Sierre: Monographic SA, 300 pp.

1405   GSCHWIND, Francisco J., 1959: *La fundación de la Colonia San Carlos y su influencia en el progreso agrícola argentino*. Santa Fe, 44 pp.

1406   OGGIER, Gabriel and Emilio B. JULLIER, 1984: *Historia de San Jerónimo Norte. Una colonia agrícola-ganadera de inmigrantes suizos en la República Argentina, vol. 1*. Rosario: Editorial Apis, 343 pp.

1407   SCHOBLINGER, Juan, 1957: *Inmigración y colonización: suizas en la República Argentina en el siglo XIX.* Buenos Aires: Instituto de Cultura Suizo-Argentino, 231 pp.

Brazil

1408   MÜLLER, J., 1972: *Die Schweizersiedlung Helvetia im Staat São Paulo.* Zurich.

1409   NICOULIN, Martin, 1973: *La genèse de Nova Friburgo. Emigration et colonisation suisse au Brésil 1817-1827.* Fribourg: Editions Universitaires, 364 pp.

1410   NICOULIN, Martin, 1976: 'Gênese de Nova Friburgo: história de uma pesquisa', *JGSWGL*, vol 13, pp. 181-188.

1411   ZIEGLER, Béatrice, 1985: *Schweizer statt Sklaven. Schweizerische Auswanderer in den Kaffee-Plantagen von São Paulo (1852-1866).* Stuttgart: Steiner, 466 pp.

1412   ZIEGLER, Béatrice, 1988: 'Schweizerische Kaufleute in Brasilien im 19. Jahrhundert', *JGSWGL*, vol. 25, pp. 141-167.

See also: 98

Chile

1413   MARTINIC, Mateo, 1975: 'La inmigración suiza en Magallanes, 1875-1890', *AIP*, 6/1-2,

1414   SCHNEITER, Frederico, 1983: *Die schweizer Einwanderung in Chile – la inmigración suiza en Chile.* Bern: Gesamtherstellung Stampfl, 219 pp.

Uruguay

1415   ANNAHEIM, Hans, 1967: 'Die Kolonie Nueva Helvecia in Uruguay', *RBS*, vol. 8, 49 pp.

1416   WIRTH, Juan Carlos, 1980: *Génesis de la colonia agrícola suiza Nueva Helvecia,* vol. 1: *Historia;* vol. 2: *Documentos y cartografía.* Montevideo: Ministerio de Educación y Cultura, vol. 1: 153 pp; vol. 2: 284 pp.

UKRAINIAN

Bibliography

1417   CIPKO, Serge, 1990: *The Ukrainian press in Latin America: a concise bibliographical survey.* Sydney: Ukrainian Studies Centre, Macquarie University (Research Report, No. 3), 19 pp.

General

1418   STRELKO, Andrei, 1975: 'Primeros inmigrantes ucranianos en Latino-américa', *AL*, no.1, pp. 89-98

1419   STRELKO, Andrei, 1980: *Slavianskoe naselenie v stranakh Latynskoi Ameriki.* Kiev: Naukova dumka.

See also: 341

Argentina

1420   BARTOLOMÉ, Leopoldo, 1975: 'Colonos, plantadores y agroindustrias: la explotación agrícola familiar en el sudeste de Misiones', *DEC*, 4/3, pp. 3-8.

1421   BARTOLOMÉ, Leopoldo, 1977: 'Sistemas de actividad y estrategias adaptativas en la articulación regional y nacional de colonias agrícolas étnicas: el caso de Apóstoles (Misiones)', *PAC*, pp. 257-281.

1422   BARTOLOMÉ, Leopoldo, 1991: *The Colonos of Apóstoles: adaptive stategy and ethnicity in a Polish-Ukrainian settlement in northeast Argentina.* New York: AMS Press.

1423   DANYLYSHYN, Mykhailo, 1979: *Ukraintsi v Argentyni. Los ucranios en la República Argentina.* Buenos Aires: Imprenta Dorrego, 392 pp.

1424   GERUS, Oleh W., 1986: 'Ukrainians in Argentina: a Canadian perspective', *JUS*, 11/2, pp. 3-18.

1425   RUDNYCKYJ, J.B., 1974: 'Canadian and Argentine-Brazilian novels on Ukrainian pioneers', *UR*, 21/4, pp. 91-96.

1426   SACIUK, Olena H., 1983: 'Ukrainian and Spanish exile writers in

Argentina', in Hans-Bernhard Moeller, ed., *Latin America and the literature of exile*. Heidelberg: Carl Winter Universitätsverlag, pp. 277-292.

1427   SZAFOVAL, Mykola, 1987: 'Die Ukrainische Ansiedlung in Argentinien', *JU*.

1428   WASYLYK, Miguel, 1985: 'La inmigración ucraniana a la Argentina', in *La inmigración a América Latina (primeras jornadas internacionales sobre la migración en América)*. México, DF: Instituto Panamericano de Geografía e Historia (serie inmigración, tomo 2), pp. 135-152.

See also: 341; 925; 1118; 1119

Brazil

1429   BORUSZENKO, Oksana, 1978: 'L'immigration ukrainienne au Brésil', *EC*, no. 35.

1430   BORUSZENKO, Oksana, 1981: *Os Ucranianos*. Curitiba: Fundação Cultural Casa Romário Martins (Boletim Informativo, 8/53), 27 pp.

1431   BURKO, Valdomiro., 1963: *A imigração ucraniana no Brasil*. Curitiba, 95 pp.

1432   CIPKO, Serge, 1986: 'The legacy of the "Brazilian Fever": the Ukrainian colonization of Paraná', *JUS*, 11/2, pp. 19-32.

1433   KULEZYNSKYJ, Wolodymyr, 1983-4: 'Mapeamento de comunidades eslavos no Paraná', *FL*, vol. 3, pp. 23-53.

1434   STAROSCHAK, Metro., 1987: 'Visiting the Ukrainian Orthodox colonies of Brazil', *FUR*, no. 70, pp. 27-30.

1435   WOUK, Miguel, 1981: *Estudo etnográfico-lingüístico da comunidade ucraína de Dorizon*. Curitiba: Secretaria da Cultura e do Esporte do Governo do Estado do Paraná.

1436   ZINKO, V., 1960: *Ridna shkola u Brazylii*. Prudentópolis: Tipografia dos Padres Basilanos.

Paraguay

1437   ZUB KURYLOWICZ, Roberto, 1984: 'Los eslavos en la historia Paraguaya', *RPS*, 21/60, pp. 183-190.

YUGOSLAV

General

1438   ANTIĆ, Ljubomir, 1986: 'Prilog istraživanju odnosa naših iseljenika u Južnoj Americi prema NOB-u s posebnim osvrtom na JNO na Pacifiku', *CSP*, 17/1, pp. 43-80.

1439   ANTIĆ, Ljubomir, 1987: *Naše iseljeništvo u Južnoj Americi stvaranje i jugoslavenske države 1918*. Zagreb: Školska Knjiga, 222 pp.

See also: 341

Argentina

1440   DAHL, Victor C., 1974: 'Yugoslav immigration experience in Argentina and Chile', *IAEA*, 28/3, pp. 3-26.

Brazil

1441   ANTIĆ, Josip, 1989: 'Jugoslavenski iseljenici u Brazilu', *MT*, 4/4, pp. 269-286.

Chile

1442   ANTIĆ, Ljubomir, 1984: 'Sukobi u jugoslavenskom iseljeničkom pokretu u Antofagasti (Čile) za vrijeme prvog svjetskog rata i neki socijalni utjecaji na njih 1917, godine', *CSP*, 16/2, pp. 19-47.

1443   BONACIĆ-DORIĆ B., Lucas, 1941: *Historia de los yugoslavos en Magallanes: su vida y su cultura*, vol. 1. Punta Arenas: Imp. "La Nacional", 248 pp.

1444   BONACIĆ-DORIĆ B., Lucas, 1943: *Historia de los yugoslavos en Magallanes: su vida y su cultura*, vol. 2. Punta Arenas: Imp. "La Nacional", 221 pp.

1445   BONACIĆ-DORIĆ B., Lucas, 1946: *Historia de los yugoslavos en Magallanes: su vida y su cultura*, vol. 3. Punta Arenas: Imp. "La Nacional", 264 pp.

1446   MARTINIĆ BEROS, Mateo, 1985, 2nd ed.: *La inmigración yugoslava en Magallanes*. Punta Arenas: Offset Rasmussen.

1447   RAJEVIĆ, Andres, 1983: 'Presencia yugoslava en Chile', *RCH*, no. 4, pp. 109-116.

See also: 1439

Peru

1448   MESELAZIĆ DE PEREYRA, Zivana, 1985: *Yugoslavos en el Perú*. Lima: Editorial La Equidad, 240 pp.

Croat

General

1449   ANTIĆ, Ljubomir, 1983: 'Pokušaj stvaranja "Hrvatskog saveza" među našim iseljenicima u Južnoj Americi 1913. godine', *CSP*, 15/2, pp. 43-62.

1450   ANTIĆ, Ljubomir, 1984: 'Pregled hrvatskih iseljeničkih društava u Južnoj Americi do prvog svjetskog rata', *RIHP*, vol. 17, pp. 121-160.

1451   ANTIĆ, Ljubomir, 1987: 'Pregled hrvatskog iseljeničkog tiska u Južnoj Americi do prvog svjetskog rata', *RIHP*, vol. 20, pp. 101-127.

1452   ANTIĆ, Ljubomir, 1988:   'Osnovne značajke hrvatskog isljeništva u španjolskoj Južnoj Americi do prvog svjetskog rata', *MT*, 4/1-2, pp. 413-437.

1453   ANTIĆ, Ljubomir, 1991: *Hrvati u Južnoj Americi do godine 1914*. Zagreb: STVARNOST and Institut za migracije i narodnosti Sveučilišta u Zagrebu, 370 pp.

Argentina

1454   ANTIĆ, Ljubomir, 1990: 'Prolegomena za raspravu o Hrvatima u Argentini do 1914', *MT*, 6/2, pp. 183-194.

1455   LUKAC DE STIER, Maja, 1986: 'Aportes de la colectividad croata a la República Argentina', *SCR*, no. 102, pp. 221-234.

See also: 925

Bolivia

1456   ANTIĆ, Ljubomir, 1986: 'Naši iseljenici u Boliviji prema NOB-i i obnovi zemlje', *MT*, 2/2, pp. 85-98.

1457   BORIĆ, Ivo, 1986: 'Los inmigrantes croatas en Bolivia', *SCR*, no. 102, pp. 235-241.

1458   LUPIS-VUKIĆ, Ivan, 1954: 'Bračani u Boliviji', *BZ*, vol. 22, pp. 176-185.

Chile

1459   ANTIĆ, Ljubomir, 1987: 'Ivan Krstulović: pokretač hrvatskog iseljeničkog tiska u Čileu', *ZR*, 36/3, pp. 227-245.

1460   ANTIĆ, Ljubomir, 1988: 'Elementi klasnog sukoba u nemirima u hrvatskoj iseljeničkoj koloniji u Antofagasti (Čili) godine 1917', *MT*, 4/4, pp. 413-437.

1461   ANTIĆ, Ljubomir, 1989: 'Sportska aktivnost u hrvatskog iseljeničkoj koloniji u Punta Arenasu (Čili) do prvog svetskog rata', *PS*, 20/80, pp. 107-110.

1462   BORIĆ, Ivo, 1978: 'Emigración croata a Chile: vida de la colonia y sus obras', *SCR*, no. 70-71, pp. 141-157.

1463   MARTINIĆ BEROS, Mateo, 1985: 'La controversia político-nacional entre los inmigrantes croatas de Magallanes (1896-1918)', *SCR*, no. 99, pp. 303-331.

1464   MARTINIĆ BEROS, Matéo, 1986: 'Los inmigrantes en Magallanes (Chile) y la cuestión croata (1919-1939), *SCR*, no. 103, pp. 320-334.

1465   POLAKOVICH, Esteban, 1981: 'La soledad étnica en la obra de Martin Kukucin. La suerte de los croatas en Punta Arenas', *SC*, no. 82-83, pp. 168-175.

Peru

1466   ANTIĆ, Ljubomir, 1984: 'Dubrovačka kolonija u Cerro de Pasco (Peru) prema pismima iseljenika zadarskom "Narodnom listu"', *DK*, 27/5-6, pp. 113-125.

Slovene

Argentina

1467   VELIKONJA, Joseph, 1985: 'Las comunidades eslovenas en el Gran Buenos Aires', *EML*, no. 1, pp. 48-61.

1468   ŽITNIK, Janja, 1990: 'Slovenskoargentinski pesnik Vinko Žitnik', *DD*, 1, pp. 275-290.

MIGRATION STUDIES CENTRES

Croatia

Institut za migracije i narodnosti
[Institute for Migration and Nationalities]
Sveucilista u Zagreb [University of Zagreb]
P.O. Box 88
Trnjanska b.b.
41000 Zagreb
[tel. (041) 539-988; 539-777]

Denmark

Det danske Udvandrerarkiv
[Danes Worldwide Archive]
Ved Vor Frue Kirke
P.O. Box 1731
9100 Aalborg
[tel. 45 98 12 57 93]

Finland

Siirtolaisuusinstituutti
[Institute of Migration]
Piispankatu 3
20500 Turku
[tel. (021) 317 536]

Germany

Institut für Auslandsbeziehungen
Charlottenplatz 17
7000 Stuttgart 1
[tel. (07 11) 2 22 50]

Italy

Centro Studi Emigrazione
Via Dandolo 58
00153 Roma
[tel. 58.09.764]

Netherlands

Emigratiebestuur
2511 VW 's-Gravenhage
Muzenstraat 30
[tel. (070) 62 46 11]

Norway

Det norsk utvandrersenteret
[The Norwegian Emigration Center]
Bergjelandsgt 30
N-4012 Stavanger
[tel. (474) 52 07 08]

Slovenia

Inštitut za slovensko izeljenstvo
[Institute for Slovene Immigration Research]
Slovenske akademije znanosti in umetnosti
[Slovene Academy of Sciences and Arts]
Novi Trg 5
61000 Ljubljana
[tel. (061) 331-021, ext. 77]

Spain

Instituto Español de Emigración
Pintor Rosales 44
Madrid 28071
[tel. 247 52 00]

Sweden

Svenska Emigrantinstitutet
[Swedish Emigrants Institute]
Box 201
S-351 04 Växjö 1
[tel. (0470) 201 20]

Argentina

Centro de Estudios Migratorios Latinoamericanos
Calle Necochea 330
1158 Buenos Aires
[tel. 334 7717]

Centro de Documentación e Información sobre Judaísmo Argentino
"Marc Turkow"
Ayacucho 632 - 3 piso
1026 Buenos Aires
[tel. 49-0518/20691]

Brazil

Centro de Estudos Migratorios
Rua Vasco Pereira 53
01415 - São Paulo - SP

Instituto Hans Staden
Rua 7 de Abril 59-4º andar
01043 - São Paulo - SP
[tel. (011) 34-3981; 34-4738]

Centro de Estudos Judaicos
Faculdade de Filosofia, Letra e Ciências Humanas
Universidade de São Paulo
05508 - São Paulo - SP

Canada

Multicultural History Society of
Ontario
43 Queen's Park Crescent, E.
Toronto, Ontario M5S 2C3

U.S.A.

Immigration History Research Center
University of Minnesota
826 Berry Street
St. Paul, Minnesota 55114
[tel. (612) 627-4208]

Center for Migration Studies
209 Flagg Place
Staten Island, NY 10304
[tel. (718) 351 8800]

AUTHOR INDEX

INSTITUTE OF LATIN AMERICAN STUDIES

RESEARCH PAPERS

No 1: Oil and Politics in Ecuador, 1972-1976 by George Philip (1978)

No 2: Industrial Investment in an 'Export' Economy: the Brazilian Experience before 1914 by Flávio Rabelo Versiani (1979)

No 3: Peruvian Labour and the Military Government since 1968 by Alan Angell (1980)

No 4: Labour in Chile under the Junta, 1973-1979 by Gonzalo Falabella (1981)

No 5: W.H. Hudson: the Colonial's Revenge. A Reading of his Fiction and his Relationship with Charles Darwin by Jason Wilson (1981)

No 6: Development Policymaking in Mexico: the Sistema Alimentario Mexicano (SAM) by Michael Redclift (1981)

No 7: Brazilian Private Industrial Enterprise, 1950-1980 by Susan M. Cunningham (1982)

No 8: Bolivia 1980-1981: the Political System in Crisis by James Dunkerley (1982)

No 9: Paraguay in the 1970s: Continuity and Change in the Political Process by James Painter (1983)

No 10: Simón Bolívar and the Age of Revolution by John Lynch (1983)

No 11: The Crisis of the Chilean Socialist Party (PSCh) in 1979 by Carmelo Furci (1984)

No 12: Bonanza Development? The Selva Oil Industry in Peru, 1968-1982 by George Philip (1984)

No 13: The Retreat from Oil Nationalism in Ecuador, 1976-1983 by Christopher Brogan (1984)

No 14: Harnessing the Interior Vote: the Impact of Economic Change, Unbalanced Development and Authoritarianism on the Local Politics of Northeast Brazil by Scott William Hoefle (1985)

No 15: Caciques, Tribute and Migration in the Southern Andes: Indian Society and the 17th Century Colonial Order (Audencia de Charcas) by Thierry Saignes (1985)

No 16: The Market of Potosí at the End of the Eighteenth Century by Enrique Tandeter (1987)

No 17: Prostitution in Nineteenth-Century Rio de Janeiro by Luiz Carlos Soares (1988)

No 18: The State and Henequen Production in Yucatán, 1955-1980 by Roberto Escalante (1988)

Papers in this series may be obtained from the
INSTITUTE OF LATIN AMERICAN STUDIES
31, Tavistock Square, London WC1H 9HA

Price per copy, including postage:

Vols 1-20
United Kingdom and Europe £3.50, Overseas (airmail) £5.00 (US $11.50)

Vols 21-
United Kingdom and Europe £4.50, Overseas (airmail) £7.00 (US $14.00)

Please make cheques payable to The University of London

AN A TO Z OF LATIN AMERICAN LITERATURE IN ENGLISH TRANSLATION

Compiled by Jason Wilson

"Say what you will of its inadequacy, translation remains one of the most important, worthwhile concerns in the totality of world affairs."

Goethe to Carlisle

****

The A to Z is a checklist and guide to the fiction, theatre and poetry (and some essays and memoirs) of the Spanish and Portuguese speaking New World since Independence: 650 published translations of works by 256 authors, from Agosín to Zurita, with an appendix of 118 Anthologies and a Bibliography of sources.

This will be a useful bibliographical tool for scholars and librarians and will give the student of comparative literature and the general reader access to the rich and important field of Latin American Literature.

About the author
Jason Wilson is Lecturer in Latin American Literature at University College London. He has published two books on Octavio Paz, and essays and reviews on Latin American literature and culture. Special interests include the translation of Alexander von Humboldt's *Travels*.

ISBN 0 901145 67 X
£5.50 UK   £7.50 Overseas (US$13.50).